"Amy's story of fa
amidst the trials
filtered through r
anchored in the Scriptures, with clear, practical action steps for the reader. May it encourage those who feel 'stuck' to press on in prayer and obedience, knowing that God can beautifully unfold His plans for their lives as well."

— Dr. John Fuder, Heart for the City,
Chicagoland United in Prayer

"No More Status Quo.
Riveting. Compelling. Inspiring. Interactive. Amy Joob is not only an action-minded, powerful prayer warrior, but the catalyst for us to move past current limitations into a life of eternal productivity and reward. Get ready to soar to new heights as you get unstuck, freed up, and launched into the life God created you to live."

— Marnie Swedberg, author, speaker & Perspective
Transforming Aha Generator, www.Marnie.com

"Have you ever felt stuck? You're not alone. Amy Joob has been there and she's ready to share with you the steps she's discovered to getting unstuck. This engaging 40-day devotional will help you break free and find biblical courage to step into the new God has for you."

— Rhonda Stoppe, No Regrets Woman,
author of 6 books including: *Moms Raising Sons to Be Men*

"Amy's rock-solid faith in God will spark renewal in your own spiritual life. Prayer is her go-to response in difficult moments and she is quick to turn to Scripture – her source for wisdom.

Part spiritual guide, part life coach, Amy not only encourages and cheers you on, she models how to seek God and trust Him in every season. Amy demonstrates that even when we feel stuck, moving towards God in faith and surrender is always the next right step."

— Becky Baudouin, speaker and author of
Enjoy Every Minute and Other Ridiculous Things We Say to Moms and *Cancer, Faith, and Unexpected Joy.*

"This book is like having a personal coach and cheerleader in your back pocket. God used Amy's inspirational stories, her "can do" attitude, and the perfect journaling prompts to resuscitate my weary heart. After a long, hard season it was just what I needed to get moving again. (Thank you, Amy, for not ignoring God's call to write this book!)"

— Liz Lassa, speaker and creator
of the *Spiritual Circle Journal*

"A must read! Amy perfectly balances insight from her past experiences along with well-crafted questions to guide and inspire you to live out the wonderful and purposeful life that God has in store for you."

— Carolyn Litton, president and founder of Hearts for Hope and creator of The Vision Project

"*Unstuck, Step Into the New* is definitely on my Christmas list! Amy uses her own unique life experiences to challenge, inspire, and instruct the reader on everyday situations and problems. Her questions help guide you to the solution. Thank you, Amy, for obeying the call to write!"

— Larry and Jean Johnson, directors of Will Go Missions

"A Must Read. Amy, a gifted life coach and encourager, in her book *Unstuck*, grabs your attention from her experiences which speak to all of us, then she inspires, instructs, and challenges all of us to be unstuck and to return as victors/ overcomers on our life's journey; always knowing in Christ, we will fulfill His purpose and achieve His divine destiny for us. Apply the appendix early in your journey."

— Eldon L. Tracy, missionary and apostle of encouragement

A 40-Day Prayer Journal

AMY ROBNIK JOOB

Copyright © 2021 by Amy Robnik Joob

All rights reserved. No part of this book may be reproduced or used in any manner without written permission of the copyright owner except for the use of quotations in a book review.

This is a work of creative nonfiction. The events and conversations in this book have been written to the best of the author's ability, but some names and details have been changed to protect the privacy of individuals.

Unless otherwise noted, all scripture is taken from The Holy Bible, New International Version®, NIV® Copyright 1973, 1978, 1984, 2011 by Biblica, Inc. The Living Bible copyright © 1971 by Tyndale House Foundation, Carol Stream, Illinois 60188. All rights reserved worldwide.

For more information, contact: amyjoob@yahoo.com

First paperback edition September 2021

Front Cover by Mindy Comincioli
Back Cover Photo by Kim King Failing
Book design by David W. Edelstein

ISBN: 978-1-7370638-0-3 (paperback)
ISBN: 978-7370638-1-0 (e-book)

www.amyjoob.com

In loving memory of Dianne Matter

Thank you for teaching Arianna the keys on piano and me the keys to prayer and being a pioneer. We will hold you in our hearts forever!

"Yet, I still belong to you; you are holding my right hand. You will keep on guiding me with your counsel; leading me to a glorious destiny."

(Psalm 73:23-24, New Living Translation, Compact Edition)

Contents

FOREWORD

A daily dose of spiritual courage!

I have known Amy for nearly three decades and it is amazing to see how she continues to press into the goodness of God and be used to advance His Kingdom. Her writing comes from a place of raw and authentic spiritual growth in her life that has been forged through much hardship and difficulty. When we think about pushing forward, sometimes we think that there is just a hurdle or two, but I have seen Amy push through hurdle after hurdle over the years and pave a path to great freedom and victory in Christ. This devotion will create a foundation in your life to begin again, to dream again, and to step out in faith again. As you read these pages you will recognize that Amy's journey has been full of good fruit, but you will also notice that this good fruit came forth through many seasons of pruning and adversity. Amy is relentless in pushing through while the enemy is trying to bring disruptions in her life and the life of her family. Her "never quit" attitude and absolute belief in the goodness of God will jumpstart you toward a deeper daily walk with Jesus.

Elissa Polley, M.A., J.D.
wife, mom, anti-trafficking advocate

INTRODUCTION

Do you need hope? Are you searching for clear direction for your future? Did you pick up this book because you are seeking the courage to take your next right step?

Perhaps your life has been turned upside down by the recent pandemic. Maybe your career has been stripped away or you are trying to move into a new season of life and work. And maybe you feel stuck or side-lined.

I have been through each of these scenarios. I know life's painful transitions, the painstaking search for the right door, and at times, the difficulty of taking the next step forward. Perhaps you're there now. One door has closed in your life, the new one hasn't opened, and you are experiencing chaos in the hallway. If that is true for you, I can relate, and I believe you will find solace and direction from God as you work through this prayer journal.

I'm glad you found your way onto these pages, and

I want you to know I have been praying for you. I hope that as you read through each day and journal, God would give you a clear vision for where He is taking you. May you find courage and strength to take the next right step toward your destiny.

I pray that you get unstuck and receive a fresh wind of faith. Instead of wandering another forty days or even another forty years in the wilderness like the Israelites (you can read the full story starting in Exodus 13), why not determine to *begin today* to move in the new direction God has for you?

Even as we learn from the example Jesus gave us by fasting and praying for forty days before He started His public ministry (see Matthew 4:1-17), I pray over these next forty days, God will awaken you, give you clear strategies, faith, and boldness as you take the next right step. I pray you have peace and assurance you are on the right path to fulfilling your destiny and purpose in Him.

As you work through this prayer journal, if you would like an additional resource to help on your journey, feel free to visit my website, www.amyjoob.com, and enter your email address in the pop-up box. You will receive a free mini-course on prayer to further guide you as you pray over these next forty days.

I pray you too can hold fast to this promise that has helped me through difficult transitions in my own life.

Maybe even write it on a sticky note and put it up on your fridge as a reminder that over these next forty days, you are entering into your Promised Land!

Don't be impatient for the Lord to act! Travel steadily along his path. He will honor you, giving you the land. You will see the wicked destroyed. (Psalm 37:34, NLT/CE)

Unstuck

Day 1

Believe in Miracles

I clasped my hand over my mouth, gasped, and froze in shock. I watched the lifeguard pull one lifeless girl and then another one out of the pool. *No!*

Immediately without thinking, I started praying out loud as my eyes stared ahead at the scene playing out before me. *These girls can't be more than five and seven years old. This can't be happening.* I felt like I was dreaming or watching a movie. Yet it was the middle of the day, during a summer heatwave. Only moments before, the pool had been packed with swimmers. Now, two girls lay unconscious, side by side on the pool deck with a growing number of lifeguards surrounding them. They were not moving, breathing, or coming to life. Tears welled up in my eyes and I swallowed the lump in my throat as I imagined being the mom of one of those children. I continued to pray out loud as if I was praying for my child and gradually with more urgency and authority. "In Jesus' name, I declare these girls will regain consciousness. They will live and not die and declare the works of the Lord in Jesus' name," I prayed and quoted scriptures.

"Mom, you are embarrassing me," Ashton said as he tugged on my arm. "We have to move back to the fence now. The lifeguard is moving everyone back, see?" I noticed our son was slowly following our daughter along with a crowd of parents and children back toward the fence, away from the pool.

As I struggled to collect my thoughts, a kind woman approached me and grabbed my hand. "Keep praying," she emboldened me as she joined with me in prayer. I noticed her on the pool deck just minutes earlier. I admired how a child skipped over and hugged her as they shared a pleasant exchange. *She's my kind of lady. I'd like to be her friend.* And now here we stood, holding hands and crying out to God to save these two young girls.

We both prayed out loud and there was still no movement. We kept praying. The CPR and other strategies they were trying weren't working. I noticed a woman came forward and she wasn't pool staff. *She must be the mom!* My heart broke for her. As we pressed on in prayer, my phone rang. It was my father-in-law, a pastor. I answered and put it on the speaker phone. "Dad, I am so glad you called. We need you to pray with us right now! We are praying for a miracle." I told him the situation and he began to pray with us.

"In Jesus' name, I command death to go NOW and I declare a miracle of healing and resurrection over both of these girls. Just as you raised Lazarus from the dead, I declare both girls will have breath in their lungs and come back to life in Jesus' name," my father-in-law prayed. My new friend and prayer partner and I agreed.

Suddenly, after five of the longest minutes of my life, the younger girl coughed up water, regained consciousness, and started to move. Praise God! We shouted and cried and continued to press on in prayer as the second girl still laid there lifeless.

An ambulance pulled up and they opened the fence. The paramedics hurriedly rushed in with a stretcher. They scooped up the lifeless girl and carried her out. My heart sank. *Is she not going to make it, Lord?* I looked at the clock. It seemed like 10 minutes had passed since they were first pulled from the water. Tears poured down my cheeks as I continued to plead with God for a miracle for the second girl.

"Attention, attention, the pool will now be closed for the day. Please gather your belongings and head to the exit. Thank you." As the announcer's voice rang over the PA, the lifeless girl on the stretcher was wheeled off the pool deck and into the ambulance. I gathered my children and our belongings and quietly shuffled with the crowd of people through the blazing sun toward the exit.

I bumped into my new friend on the way out. "My name is Catherine Vandy, by the way." I introduced myself as well and learned Mrs. Vandy was a teacher at an area elementary school. Her son was also the manager at the pool. She leaned over to whisper in my ear.

"I just talked to my son. She made it! The girl in the ambulance, came to in there. They haven't announced it officially yet, but I wanted you to know. Our prayers worked!" She smiled at me real big, I breathed a sigh of relief and it felt like the weight of the world fell off my shoulders. I smiled back and, dripping with sweat and tears, we gave each other a high five.

What kind of miracle are you believing in God for today? **Mark 11:23 (New King James Version)** says, **"For assuredly, I say to you, whoever says to this mountain, 'Be removed and be cast into the sea,' and does not doubt in his heart, but believes that those things he says will be done, he will have whatever he says."** With God all things are possible!

As you journal today, write down the seemingly impossible thing (s) that you would like to see God do. After you write them down, pray for God to give you a key verse in Scripture. Write down the verse and pray it

out loud over your situation. Find someone to share this situation with, and pray and believe together for God to move mountains and do the impossible in your life!

Journal & Pray

God, I am weary and discouraged, but please renew my faith and help me to believe again. I pray You will move this mountain (s) and turn this situation (s) around.

____

____

____

Thank You, God, for teaching me to build up my faith in You. Thank You for showing me a key Scripture I can stand on to believe for a miracle in my life. (Some examples are Mark 11:23, Luke 1:37, Matthew 19:26, Luke 18:27, Mark 10: 27, Mark 11:24, Matthew 21:22, and Matthew 18:19.)

____

____

____

Day 2

Dream Again

Have recent events knocked you out? Do you feel like you are not worthy to do something great again?

Maybe you lost your job or your career due to the pandemic, or you have gone through some major life-changing experience like a divorce or long-term health crisis. I can relate. A few years back, our son Ashton was diagnosed with a genetic condition called Noonan Syndrome. It took us nearly two years, numerous specialists, and many doctors to get a grasp on his condition. And then when the pandemic hit in 2020, all live events were canceled, and both my husband and I were left without work for months. He had just started a new production company the year before, and it felt like we had to start all over again.

If you have experienced something similar, I want to encourage you to give yourself permission to dream again. Maybe you were raised in a crazy environment, or you were told you would never amount to anything. Or maybe a coach, boss, or ex spoke negatively to you about the one thing you hoped to accomplish in life. If you feel like you are knocked down and out and are just sitting in the stands as a spectator, I want to invite you back into the game. It's time to get up out of your seat and get back into the action.

Give yourself permission to dream again, and go for your goal. Know that God is ultimately your coach, and if you give your life to Him, He will make all things new. **"Behold, I will do a new thing, now it shall spring forth; shall you not know it? I will even make a road in the wilderness and rivers in the desert." (Isaiah 43:19, NKJV)**

God promises us in His word that He will make all things new. And He is a God of second chances and career re-launches. His grace is sufficient for you. He won't renege on His offer or the vision He gave you because you messed up or someone hurt you. It's time to get up again. It's time to take the next step forward. The first step is believing that good things are going to happen. Dream. Believe. Try.

Today, as you pray and journal, write down big dreams. The sky is the limit. What one thing have you always wanted to do? Be an author? Own your own business? Start a non-profit? Go back to school? If time constraints, money, or family commitments weren't an issue, what would you do? Write down your vision and give yourself permission to believe in the impossible. Make sure to include as many details as possible. Pray that God does a new work in you and that you can see yourself through His eyes and see yourself accomplishing your vision. I believe God is birthing a new vision in you and this is how to take the first step toward your new season and Promised Land.

"Write the vision and make it plain on tablets, that he may run who reads it. For the vision is yet for an appointed time; But at the end it will speak, and it will not lie. Though it tarries, wait for it; because it will surely come, it will not tarry." (Habakkuk 2:2-3, NKJV)

Journal & Pray

Dream big! Write the vision and make it clear (find extra space to write if need be). If time, money, family commitments, and other responsibilities were not on my plate, I would like to . . .

____

____

____

To see this vision come to pass and this goal to take shape, I will need to: (go back to college, take a class, read a book, find a coach . . .).

____

____

____

Day 3

The Call

I took a leap of faith and left my full-time job managing the teen center.

Eric and I were recently married, and we were on opposite work schedules. I injured my back, which in turn ended my triathlon career and the increasing stress of management led to my leap of faith. I also sensed that God was calling me to something bigger.

After graduating from Christian Life College with a degree in Pastoral Studies, I had the heart to reach young people. I wanted to share the Gospel of Jesus Christ with hurting people in the world. After much soul searching and a few divine appointments, it became clear to me that God was calling me to bring His love into the modeling industry.

Within the first few months of pursuing my modeling career, I saw a segment on the news that intrigued me and thought it might be something I should pursue. I picked up the phone and dialed my friend.

"Jessica, what is a casting call?"

I paused on the phone to hear the response from my actor friend.

"Well, it's like an audition. You try out for a role. I think it has to do with television or the movies."

"Yes, you are right. I was just watching WGN News and the anchor said a casting call will be held for Oceans 11 soon in Chicago. I was thinking . . . maybe I should go?"

"Amy, you totally should! You are pursuing modeling but acting jobs would be great to get too."

With the vote of confidence from Jessica, I decided to go on my first casting call. It was only for an extra position, but I was knocking on as many doors as possible.

I needed to pray and exercise my faith. **". . . Truly I tell you, if you have faith as small as a mustard seed, you can say to this mountain, 'Move from here to there,' and it will move. Nothing will be impossible for you." (Matthew 17:20)**

Thankfully, I was selected from the hopefuls and given details for the job. The night before the job, I dreamt that I met Matt Damon and was positioned next to him on set and offered a line. I was completely starstruck and couldn't deliver my line. I heard the director shout, "Next!"

As I drove to work the following day, I prayed that I wouldn't lose my composure if I met any celebrities and that I could remember and deliver my lines. I didn't want to screw up a good thing.

The morning slowly marched on, and lunch came and went. Finally, I heard my name being called. As I made my way out onto the street, one of the assistants on set motioned for me and another woman to come over and he placed us next to a stand-in. We smiled at each other, and our eyes grew like saucers as we watched Matt Damon walk across the street and stand right next to us.

And thankfully, because of my dream, I didn't blow it! I was able to make small talk and do my part that day. I didn't get offered a line, but I held my composure and followed the directions I was given. Standing there, I felt God not only confirm my call to be in the industry but also the reassurance He would prepare me and walk with me as I took steps of faith.

Has God asked you to step out into something huge? Do you feel unqualified and insecure because it is unfamiliar to you? I want to encourage you today—God often calls us into something that feels much bigger than we can handle. Take time to journal today, and tell Him

about your fears, concerns, doubts, and insecurities. Ask Him to fill you with boldness and courage to step out in the direction He is leading you.

Journal & Pray

The fears, doubts, concerns, and insecurities I have about moving toward my dreams and goals are . . .

____

____

____

God, I feel You are calling me to . . .

____

____

____

Day 4

Steward the Vision

I sat in the basement with the dog nestled beside me and laid out my pictures and magazine clippings on the floor. I recently left my full-time job to pursue a full-time career in professional modeling. I was listed with one agency and only had a handful of jobs under my belt, yet I sensed God had a much bigger plan in mind for my future and my career.

And so I wrote down the goals, dreams, and vision I had for my modeling career and sat down to make a vision board of what I hoped would transpire in the future. With glue stick in hand, I began to paste my headshot and photos from the jobs I had worked as well as words on my board of what I hoped was to come.

I then hung the board over my desk so I could see it daily and pray God would bring the dream to even greater fruition. Stewarding the vision God gave me became my most urgent goal. You may ask, "What does 'steward' mean and how does it relate to what God is calling us to do?" According to the Holman Bible Dictionary, stewardship is defined as "utilizing and managing all resources God provides for the glory of God and the betterment of His creation."[1] I believe each of us has unique gifts, talents, and abilities given by God. He wants us to use those for His glory and to use the financial resources He provides to help bless others and to further His Kingdom.

After I placed my vision board on the wall, I got out my index card and wrote **Matthew 7:7–8** on top: "**Ask, and it will be given to you; seek and you will find; knock and the door will be opened to you. For everyone who asks receives; the one who seeks finds; and to the one who knocks, the door will be opened.**" And under that verse, I wrote down three goals in modeling I prayed would come to pass, and I taped it up on my bathroom mirror.

If you hope to see your dream turn into a reality you need to start with a clear vision. We have to "see" the dream come to pass before it does. We need to keep the vision before us daily and commit it to prayer. As you journal today, think about the dream and vision you wrote down yesterday. What are three main things you hope to see come to pass regarding the vision God has given you? Take time to get out a small piece of paper or a 3 x 5 index card and write Matthew 7:7–8 at the top. Then list the three goals you pray will come to pass. Tape it up somewhere you can see it every day. Pray that God helps you bring these goals to pass. It may seem out of your reach, but that is where God can show up, meet you in your weakness, and do the impossible through you.

Journal & Pray

As I read through the dream and vision God gave me (on Day 1), the three goals I believe I will accomplish with His help are:

1. ______________________________

2. ______________________________

3. ______________________________

On my index card, I am writing down Matthew 7:7–8, listing these three goals and taping them up on ____________ to encourage and build my faith each day.

Day 5

Finish Line in Sight

"Amy, grab Arianna! You can cross the finish line together!"

Eric's voice rang out among the crowd in Dallas as I ran down the final stretch of the White Rock Marathon. I sauntered over, took Arianna, and whispered a prayer I would have the strength to carry our ten month old daughter the last several yards over the finish line. My legs felt like spaghetti noodles from running 26 miles and I tried not to buckle to the ground as I pressed forward with my smiling daughter in my arms.

Visualizing the finish line during the race is what kept a smile on my face. We crossed the finish line together, and I put my medal around her neck in the finisher's chute. We smiled for pictures, and I thanked God that He helped me to finish strong.

Running began early for me, during my elementary

years when I was around 10 or 11 years old. The sense of accomplishment I felt after a run and the way it cleared my mind, kept me thinking positively and kept me running. Pushing myself past my limitations led me from running cross country and track in high school to competing in triathlons (run, bike, and swim) during my college years and then on to half and full marathons. One race built on another and the experience of training, setting goals, and completing races taught me you can reach for the impossible and achieve it if you prepare, train, and believe.

"Therefore I tell you, whatever you ask for in prayer, believe that you have received it, and it will be yours" (Mark 11:24) is the verse I held onto as I ran the marathon in Dallas and have held onto during challenges in life since then.

Whether you are facing a challenge, working toward finishing your college degree, earning your certification as an esthetician or realtor, launching your first business, or training for your first marathon, I want to encourage you not to give up. Keep imagining yourself completing your goal and thank God in advance for the strength to finish and to see your dream come to pass.

Take time to journal today and pray that God gives you a renewed strength and motivation to move forward. Pray that He gives you an ability to "see" yourself in faith completing the vision and successfully crossing the finish line. As you journal today, think of one action step you can take toward the three goals you wrote down yesterday. And pray about one person you can ask to pray with you and keep you accountable as you move forward with the goals He has given you. You will get to the finish line and cross over, one step at a time. Be encouraged and don't give up!

Journal & Pray

The one action step I can take today to move onto the right path toward my goal is . . .

___

___

___

The one person I plan to ask to pray for me as I take this next right step is . . .

___

___

___

Day 6

Trust As You Wait

The snow fell softly that January day as I eagerly awaited the results of my MRI.

After finishing my second of two marathons that year, my back was screaming at me. The bike and car accidents during my twenties combined with the marathons brought me to the doctor's office.

The chiropractor walked in, "Well, how do you feel? Do you even want me to tell you the results?"

"Yes," I said, bracing to hear the truth as I saw a look of concern darken her eyes. "This shows you have bulging disks at L-3, L-4, and L-5 and I am seeing arthritis and an issue with S-1 too."

Yikes! Not exactly how you want to start your new year. I had to rest, walk, and go to many decompression sessions. Following the weeks of going to these appointments, I then saw a physical therapist for additional rehab. I felt like God was forcing me to slow down in that season and focus on writing. I complied and kept pounding on the keys of my laptop until I found an editor through my friend. Over the next couple of years, I felt like an apprentice as my editor taught me how to write and helped me shape my memoir.

It was a painful season in my life, emotionally and physically. There were many doctors and treatments, many ups and downs, many hours clunking away at keys with multiple revisions and drafts. During this season I clung to **Psalm 37:34 (NLT/CE), "Don't be impatient for the Lord to act. Travel steadily along his path. He will honor you, giving you the land. You will see the wicked destroyed."** I trusted God was working behind the scenes and that He was healing my body as I visited doctors and therapists. I trusted my editor and kept working toward finishing my book even when things looked impossible.

During this season of surrender and waiting for my healing, I relinquished my dreams and athletic goals once again. While waiting on Him, I focused on praying for my family more and praying for others. I began to trust God's plan for my life was the best plan after all. I grew closer to God, and I developed an increased passion to help others who were in need.

Have you been there? Are you in a season now where

you are waiting for God to bring healing or your dreams to pass? If so, I want to encourage you to keep on trusting Him. Keep trusting even when it doesn't make sense, even when you feel like you can't see light at the end of the tunnel.

As you journal today, tell God how you feel. Let Him know your frustrations, your fears, your worries, and your doubts. He understands your weariness. He has big shoulders, and He can handle everything you have to share. As you journal today, be honest with Him and share what's really going on. Then ask Him to help you to see the big picture once again. Ask for motivation and stamina to keep moving forward. He will meet you at your place of weakness, and He will strengthen you where you need Him most.

Journal & Pray

The frustrations, fears, and worries I want to lay down today are . . .

____

____

____

I am trusting God during the waiting and what I hope to see moving forward is . . .

____

____

____

Day 7

Not Stuck Forever

Ashton toddled over to me at the library and handed me a large print book.

The red cover caught my eye as I read the title, *My Father at 100,* a memoir written by Ron Reagan about his famous Dad. *Read this book. Start reading again.*

It was early 2011, and I was seeking God for direction. Our son was born with health issues and already had two surgeries under his belt at the age of two. Our daughter Arianna was six and a brilliant student. After realizing earning a master's degree or working full time was out of the question, I surrendered to His plan for my life. When I read about Ronald Reagan, it seemed like his various life experiences shaped him and prepared him to be the president. It wasn't necessarily a traditional path to the presidency, but one that God used to prepare him perfectly, nonetheless. I knew God had a perfect way to shape me for my future career in writing and speaking, too. My calling during that season was to embrace raising my two young children. I needed to be there for them, to help Arianna continue to flourish in school and to help Ashton thrive and get healthy.

Since I was at home, I embraced the "Three R's" as my goal. I decided to read 100 books (autobiographies, memoirs, and biographies), write my own life story, and run another marathon for charity. Although none of these paid me a salary upfront, I believe God wanted me to build a foundation for the next steps in my life.

I planned to finish the goals by the time Ashton was five or in kindergarten. Fortunately, he started kindergarten at six, so it gave me more time to complete them. I ran a marathon for Team in Training at Disney World and a marathon for Team World Vision in Chicago the same year. And I finished reading 100 books sometime during Ashton's kindergarten journey. Writing my book and publishing it took quite a bit longer than anticipated. It felt wonderful to have goals to shoot for while I was home parenting, working trade shows, commuting to the city, and running the kids to activities. I was doing something for myself and moving forward in life.

As a mom, you may question if God remembers that you still have dreams—not just dreams for your family, but personal dreams. I went through seasons where I had to put my children and my husband first, as it was the best thing for our family at the time. Years ago, I intentionally cut back on work and travel so I could manage the house, Ashton's Noonan Syndrome diagnosis, doctor visits, and Arianna's and Ashton's activities. You may wonder if the sacrifices will pay off and if God will still open doors for your dreams too? If you are in the throes of parenting young children or managing a major health crisis, I encourage you to hold onto **Galatians 6:9: "Let us not become weary in doing good, for at the proper time we will reap a harvest if we do not give up."**

God sees where you are at and what you are going through. He sees what you do that goes unnoticed and what you do behind the scenes. He cares and is working behind the scenes on your behalf too. Take time to journal today and let Him know how you feel. If you are overwhelmed or hurting, it's okay, He understands. Give yourself permission to write, pour out your heart, and listen to what God says to you in return. Revisit some previous entries in this prayer journal to see what God has revealed on your journey thus far. Take time today to look at pictures from your past and celebrate God's faithfulness and provision in your life. As you gain His perspective on your situation, I believe you will gain fresh motivation to carry on.

Journal & Pray

God, sometimes I question how I will get unstuck and move forward from the place I am in. I want to share my heart with You today about . . .

____

____

____

I feel overwhelmed and concerned about . . .

____

____

____

I know You have promised that You are working all things together for my good and I believe You are working behind the scenes. As I journal and pray, I want to thank You for Your provision in the past and how You have shown Yourself faithful to me and my family in these areas . . .

____

____

____

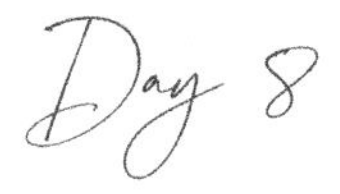

Bottom Falls Out

The burgundy carpet and gold, Victorian decor paved the path as I made my way from the hotel to the convention center in Grand Rapids.

I got there early to set up before the first customers would arrive. My mental to-do list swirled through my mind as I prayed for a successful day as a fitness model and product specialist for Met-Rx, selling protein bars at a convenience store show. My cell phone rang and interrupted my thoughts . . .

"Mom?" I chirped into my phone as I walked through the doors and onto the show floor.

"Amy, I want to let you know. I do have cancer. It's uterine cancer."

I nearly froze in place as I gulped and swallowed hard. How do you respond to such crushing news, especially when you are walking into your job? To top it off, I was working alone that day—I had no choice but to fight back tears, say a prayer, and press on.

A billow of emotions washed over me as I set up my table. **Isaiah 43:2** popped into my mind: **"When you pass through the waters, I will be with you; and when you pass through the rivers, they will not sweep over you. When you walk through the fire, you will not be burned; the flames will not set you ablaze."**

Somehow, I muddled through the day and managed to finish out the show. I sent a quick text after the initial phone call to some prayer partners, so I could start a prayer chain for my mom. Thankfully, God heard our prayers! As the days turned into weeks and the weeks turned into months, my mom pressed on in her fight to overcome cancer. She had a hysterectomy and eventually went on to have radiation treatments. With my dad at her side, she soldiered on and made it to all her appointments. She fought to get well, and I fought for her recovery on my knees in prayer. My mom said it was one of the hardest battles she ever fought in her life, but nearly a year after her original diagnosis, she was cancer-free and has been in remission for years since. Thank God!

When you receive devastating news, sometimes it feels like the world is crashing against you and all hell is breaking loose. Life continues to move forward around you, but it feels as though you are stuck in time, caught up in pain, and paralyzed by grief. It may feel as if you are frozen in place, unable to move forward like a giant obstacle is blocking your way. It's at those times that you have to cry out to God, ask him to meet you in your place of pain, and ask others to pray you through. I think it's important to give yourself permission to grieve and process through the myriad of emotions. Ask God to meet you in your dark place and ask Him to strengthen you. Ask Him to help you get through the next five minutes, to breathe, to make it through the next hour. Look for the next right step and take it.

My mom pushed past the obstacles on her way to healing, and on the other side of that enormous wall of resistance was her breakthrough. My mom realized the key to victory was in fully surrendering to Him, gaining strength from pushing against the resistance, and trusting God through the battle. The same keys can bring you victory too.

As you journal today, write down the obstacles you are currently facing. Maybe it's a financial hardship, a relationship difficulty, or a health diagnosis for you or a loved one. Or maybe it's a struggle in your marriage or a setback in your business. I want to encourage you to be completely honest with God, to journal your feelings and concerns, and give your burdens to Him. As you journal, pray that He speaks to your specific situation and gives you the grace to process through your grief. I pray God gives you a strategy and action steps to move you past the pain and obstacles you are facing today. Is there someone you can join forces with who can help pray you through?

My prayer for you is that you have an abundance of God's grace, renewed strength, fresh strategies, and the right prayer partners to pray you through. May God give you the grace to get back up and push past whatever is pressing on you. I pray you will see healing and breakthrough come to pass soon!

Journal & Pray

God, today I am facing this hardship, and I feel . . .

____

____

____

God, please speak to me. Give me a strategy and an action step I can take today to push past the pain and the obstacles. I sense You are telling me to . . .

____

____

____

These are the people I can ask for help today . . .

____

____

____

Day 9

Power in Community

I hung up the phone and fought back tears.

The customer service rep at FedEx just told me Ashton's growth hormone medication would be delayed again. The meds were grounded in Indianapolis due to a mechanical failure on the plane. I made countless phone calls over the last two weeks to ensure he would receive his meds on time. He had missed two doses already and now the arrival date could be three days away. My heart sank. Crying was out of the question since I was putting on makeup for a video interview I was filming for an upcoming event.

And then it hit me. This scene was all too familiar. It had been exactly three years since Ashton was diagnosed with Noonan Syndrome. I stood at this same sink, applying my makeup when the call came in from Dr. Ganan

Soto. You know when the doctor calls you directly, it is something serious.

"Amy, I just want to let you know we received the results of Ashton's genetic test. It is just like we suspected—he has Noonan Syndrome. The good news is he has PTPN11, the mild form, and his body will respond well to growth hormone. . ."

A tidal wave of emotion washed over me. Tears began to form as I struggled to focus on what she was saying. Her voice nearly trailed off as a million questions bombarded my mind. I laid my makeup brush on the sink, clutched the counter, and closed the door. The endocrinologist continued to explain his condition, and I willed myself to be strong. As the conversation ended, I hung up the phone, looked into the mirror, and gave myself a pep talk. *You need to pull it together to make this video. You told your agent you would have it to her today. Stay strong, you need this job, especially if Ashton has Noonan Syndrome.*

So I finished my primping and gave Eric a quick call to share the news. Promising myself I would fully process this news later, I said a prayer and used the diagnosis as my motivation to make the video for my agent. Then finally, the tears came flowing like a dam bursting forth with waters raging.

And with tears streaming, I reached out to my prayer

partner Judi and then to other family and friends who were praying. In the midst of receiving some of the hardest news of my life, I collapsed into God's presence and leaned on others for strength. A few hours after the phone call from Dr. Ganan Soto, Eric and I drove to our small group from church. We were able to process in the car and then with the other couples in our group. They extended love, empathy, and support and prayed for us and Ashton. They stood with us as we began a new, life-altering journey. **Ecclesiastes 4:10 (NLT)** says, **"If one person falls, the other can reach out and help. But someone who falls alone is in real trouble."**

There is strength and power in community. We all need others, especially during the unexpected trials and extreme challenges of life. When we come together, share openly, and pray for one another, we can find new strength, fresh perspective, and experience God's love on a deeper level. We need to celebrate each other on our mountain tops and walk with each other through our deepest, darkest valleys. There is a saying in Team World Vision, "We go farther together." If we want to walk in the complete purpose God has for us and fulfill our goals, we need to walk with others in community and help each other along the way.

My prayer is for you to be surrounded by a supportive community too. Take time to journal and ask God to bring the right alignment into your life. As you evaluate your network, you can seek out people who are of equal maturity to encourage you, some with more maturity to challenge and mentor you, and others with less experience so you can mentor them too. Ask God where He wants you to plug into community during this season of your life.

Journal & Pray

My most urgent needs right now are . . .

____

____

____

Where I could use support during this season of my life is . . .

____

____

____

The group or network I will check out, where I feel God leading me is. . .

____

____

____

Day 10

Embrace Failure

I fell down the steps off the runway.

Moments before, I lifted the skirt of my heavy, ornate wedding gown and attempted to gracefully walk off the stage, but my heel caught, and I tumbled down the stairs. Thankfully I landed on my backside and didn't get hurt. Unfortunately, the heel broke on my shoe and the incident wounded my pride.

Strut Productions was producing a show, and I was modeling bridal gowns with several others at an event in Chicago. My cheeks were burning as I limped off the side stage. I put all the weight onto the ball of my foot to walk with the broken heel until I could survey the damage backstage. I tried to laugh it off, but I was embarrassed. It was the first fall I had taken in the modeling industry, on or off the runway. *Well, there's a first time for everything.* Suddenly, videos of successful models wiping out on the runway played through my mind as I realized even the pros stumble and fall.

Summoning up my courage, I searched my model bag for another pair of heels and quickly moved to my next gown. Even though I stumbled, there were still more runs, more bridal gowns to show, and more work to be done. I had to push past the embarrassment and people's laughter and go out again. Determined to hold my head up high, I stood tall and walked the runway with a resolved smile and a little more caution.

Isaiah 41:10 admonishes us, **"So do not fear, for I am with you; do not be dismayed, for I am your God. I will strengthen you and help you, I will uphold you with my righteous right hand."**

Often the fear of failure or falling again in an area keeps us frozen, and we can't seem to move forward. Even if we have failed previously, God asks us to get up and try again. We may resist the very place of our failure because it is painful to return there, but God doesn't see our failure as a negative thing or an obstacle to avoid. Rather, our failures teach us how to do things correctly and bring us in alignment with His will and ways. Our failures strengthen and prepare us to achieve the very promises and purpose He has for us. Don't see failure as permanent, but rather as a stepping-stone to your future victory and as a tool that will enable you to reach your goal.

Is there an area in your life where God is asking you to step out or step into again? Is a current or past failure holding you back? What effects have seeped into your life due to the failure? It is important to remember that your failure is not who you are. It does not define you. As you journal and pray, name the failure, and give it to God. Know that as you give your failure to Him, it is detached from you and your identity. Ask God to reveal who you are from His perspective. Take time to reflect on your identity in Him (see appendix), and know this is how He sees you. He doesn't see your failure after you confess it to Him, He sees you through the cross of Jesus Christ. He sees you as a beloved overcomer, a new creation, a whole person, a forgiven, victorious warrior. He wants you to see yourself that way too.

Journal & Pray

The failure that is holding me back is . . .

The effects of this in my life are . . .

My identity is ultimately found in Jesus. He has forgiven me and made all things new. As I reflect on this today, I need to remember that in Him, I am . . .

Day 11

Fast and Follow Through

A big decision was in the works, and I needed to hear from God.

Returning from the Write-To-Publish conference after pitching my first manuscript led me to the crossroads of choosing the right publisher. All this was new to me, and a myriad of information swirled through my mind like a gathering windstorm. I took solace in the words of Letitia Suk, the designated chaplain at the conference. "Amy, you know there is more than one way to publish a book. Just like there is more than one way to have a baby. You can have a baby naturally, by surrogate, by in-vitro fertilization, or through adoption. In the same way, you can self-publish, publish through an indie publisher, or through a traditional publisher."

As I came home from the conference, my mind was churning as I considered my options. *Which route is best for me and my first book?* I yearned to hear His still, small voice so I could move forward confidently in the right direction. It was time to do a Daniel Fast and pray.

In **Daniel 10:2–3 (NKJV)** we read, "**In those days, I, Daniel, was mourning three full weeks. I ate no pleasant food, no meat or wine came into my mouth, nor did I anoint myself at all, till three whole weeks were fulfilled.**" This was right before Daniel had his final vision, and he was mourning for his people and his country. The Son of God appeared to Daniel, strengthened him, and gave him prophecy regarding the future of his nation.

I believe fasting can remove the confusion, help you focus on Him, and enable you to hear the voice of God more clearly. It is during these times of consecration that you are strengthened spiritually and can hear from God as He reveals His plans to you. He can do this through His Word, dreams, and visions. Fasting can give you the clarity, direction, and courage you need, not only for yourself but for those around you too.

A short time after the fast, God made the answer and direction clear. I was visiting my family in Minnesota and enjoying some time relaxing by the lake. One name kept surfacing, Redemption Press, and I felt such an overwhelming peace they were the right one to pursue. Since they are an independent publisher, I would need the financing to publish and see my first manuscript come to life.

It had been nearly seven years since I started this writing journey and I questioned if I would ever get to the finish line. After several informative talks with the CEO, affirmation, and a payment plan set in place, I stepped out in faith. I didn't know how it would all come together in the natural, yet I knew God was in it, and He was clearly leading me.

After collaborating with Redemption Press for six months, while working and caring for children, *Model Behavior: Make Your Career Path Your Calling* launched on January 28, 2019. Two months later we paid off the credit card. God worked out a publishing miracle.

Take time to journal today and ask God if He is calling you to fast and pray to see a breakthrough or receive clear direction. (Two books I suggest for more insight on this topic are *Fasting* and *The Fasting Edge* by Jentezen Franklin.) Write down your burning questions, the areas you desperately need to see God move, and the direction you are seeking. Then take time to write down the responses and impressions you get from Him. Make sure to follow through on what He is leading you to do.

Journal & Pray

God, I desire to see breakthrough and direction in . . .

____

____

____

The questions I have for You and the place I need to see You move is . . .

____

____

____

God, show me if You are calling me to fast and pray. What type of fast are You calling me to and for how long?

____

____

____

Day 12

Hear His Whisper

"Hi, this is Bob Goff here. How can I help you?"

I couldn't believe my ears. An hour before I had called Bob, he responded with an email and asked me to give him a call. And when I called, he answered. For weeks after reading his book, *Love Does,* I kept hearing a persistent voice, like a whisper, *Call Bob Goff. Call Bob Goff. He'll tell you what to do.* I finally found the courage to make the call, and I chided myself for not doing it sooner.

During the next twenty minutes, I told Bob about my book being finished, about our current work and financial situation, about our son Ashton's recent Noonan Syndrome diagnosis, and questions I had regarding the next steps in publishing.

"Well, Amy, it comes down to this. Do you want to play intramural softball or major league baseball? This is the difference between self-publishing and looking for an established publisher. It sounds like with everything you have going on with your son, you may need to find a traditional publisher. And if you want to have a writing career and make money, it's definitely the way to go."

Jeremiah 33:3 (NKJV) says, **"Call to Me, and I will answer you, and show you great and mighty things, which you do not know."** Sometimes the answer God has for you is just one phone call away.

I prayed for God to give me direction and answers regarding publishing for several weeks. I kept hearing His still, small voice but I didn't act on it right away. Finally, I mustered up some courage and made the call.

How often are we praying for answers and crying out to God over and over and when He gives us the answer, we ignore what He says? It seemed a little crazy for me to call Bob Goff. *He's not going to want to talk to me, he doesn't even know me. He probably won't even answer my call.* Yet, once I stepped out in faith and followed God's direction, I got the answers I had been searching for all along.

After that conversation, I found the courage to register and go to my first writing and publishing conference. I met my publisher there, and it was like a divine appointment. Although they are an independent publisher, they were exactly what I needed to publish my first book. I still hope to publish through a traditional publisher someday and truly believe God will lead me there step by step.

Is there an area in your life where you feel stuck? Is there something you have been praying about for a long time? What do you hear or sense God is leading you to do? Take time to listen as you write down not only the problem you are seeking a solution for but also the words you hear God speaking to your heart. As He reveals to you the next steps, I dare you to courageously move forward. You may be pleasantly surprised.

As you journal today, take time to write down each of the problems you have been facing. After you write each problem down, prayerfully ask God for direction. Listen and write down the promptings or the responses you get in your prayer time. What individuals, books, courses, or solutions is He leading you to? As you write down each problem and each solution, prayerfully ask God which one you should start on first and then courageously take the next right step.

Journal & Pray

For example:

Problem	Mentor, Person, Text, or Course
Mortgage too high	Sign up for Financial Peace University by Dave Ramsey
Health struggles with food/diet	Meet with a dietician or nutritionist
Need direction with writing/ publishing	Find an editor to work with on the book

1. ______________________________. ______________________________.

2. ______________________________. ______________________________.

3. ______________________________. ______________________________.

4. ______________________________. ______________________________.

5. ______________________________. ______________________________.

Day 13

Spread Kindness Everywhere

Give her the $20 in your pocket. This is a thankless job. I walked into the bathroom at O'Hare Airport in Chicago and I took in the lady sweeping out the stalls and dumping garbage into the large rolling trash can next to her. *I know what this feels like.* Years earlier, I had my own cleaning business on the side when I was breaking into modeling. I walked over and handed the young woman the cash from my pocket. "Thank you for all your hard work. I know this isn't easy . . . Keep up the good job!"

I felt compelled to bless this stranger and let her know her hard work was not in vain. I noticed her and, more importantly, God noticed her. I had once been in her shoes as I, too, cleaned other people's houses, apartments, and floors. As I cleaned toilets and kitchen sinks,

I prayed for the homeowners, my husband, and for God to open doors for me in the modeling industry. I made the most of it by listening to Christian radio and praying as I cleaned. I felt a certain solace cleaning and praying as it was quite the contrast from the stress and busyness I experienced managing the teen center.

As I reflected on my cleaning days, my heart swelled with gratitude for how God answered my prayers and provided contracts with Porsche Cars North America and with Met-Rx Sports Nutrition. My desire was to give back and be a blessing. God had blessed me with agents and clients that treated me well, and I wanted to bless others in return.

While traveling and modeling over the years, I looked for people to shower with mercy. I wanted to share God's love and kindness as I knew it was the main reason He called me into the business. A Christian speaker on the radio said, "God wants us to show kindness to everyone, from the janitor to those in jail, to the people at the top and everyone in between." He sees all our acts of kindness and blesses us for our efforts. **Matthew 6:3–4** says, **"But when you give to the needy, do not let your left hand know what your right hand is doing, so that your giving may be in secret. Then your Father, who sees what is done in secret, will reward you."** I purposely looked for people to bless that could never pay me back in return. And over the years, people have unexpectedly blessed me and my family in ways we could never pay back either. God works in amazing and mysterious ways!

On my very first big modeling job, I shared the love of God with my team. I was hired to do theatrical runway shows across the U.S. for Sally's Beauty Supply. Two other girls and I were the "Face of Sally's," and with distinct mime-type make-up, donning red catsuits, we slinked across the stage between the dancers at each performance. We traveled with a team of nine other women and my goal on the multi-city, hair show tour was to get to know each model/dancer, share my testimony with her, and be a source of encouragement. It helped me to focus on others and forget about my worries and insecurities as we worked at each show. By the end of the tour our choreographer, John, handed out awards. "And now our Miss Congeniality Award goes to . . . Amy Joob!"

It pays to be kind. The biggest reward for showing kindness is the warm feeling you get inside when you know you helped meet a need at the exact right time and place. I receive more joy in my life by giving than by receiving. Giving can lift you out of anxiety and discouragement and help you see your circumstances in a whole new way. Who is God prompting you to show kindness to today? Take some time to journal and write down the people you want to bless and ways you can show them kindness this week.

Journal & Pray

People/Places to bless	Action	Date to be completed	Finished?
Friend	Make video for her online business	Today	Done!
Local Food Pantry	Shop & drop off groceries	First day of next month	

Day 14

God is My Boss

"Amy, I think you need to start setting your timer for an hour each day; sit down and write until your timer goes off."

My friend Terre gave me the perfect solution! I was getting weary from writing and re-writing my manuscript. Talking with Terre in our church that day was a lightbulb moment. I took her advice and began to write an hour each day, in the same place and at the same time. I turned my phone to silent, set the timer, and prayed for God to guide me and for His words and wisdom to flow through me. This formula helped me through the rest of my memoir writing journey.

Colossians 3:23–24 says, "**Whatever you do, work at it with all your heart, as working for the Lord, not for human masters, since you know that you will**

receive an inheritance from the Lord as a reward. It is the Lord Christ you are serving."

During those long hours of solitude as the kids were at school and Eric was at work, I sat at the computer and typed and re-wrote passages and paragraphs. Often the timer would go off and I would keep typing because I was in a creative flow.

I did not have a manager or boss dictating to me what needed to be done, and I didn't have a paycheck waiting at the end of the week. Even as I prayed for the right words and for the people to read my book someday, I constantly evaluated if my writing would benefit my readers. My goal was to inspire others with my story so they, too, would fulfill the purpose and plan God had for their lives.

At times I felt bombarded with fiery arrows of self-doubt. Not only did I question my ability to write and publish a book that others would want to read, but I wondered whether or not it would even pay off in the end. *Will anyone benefit from reading my story? Should I be out working right now instead?*

And then all my doubts and questions were suddenly interrupted and silenced by His still, small voice. *"Amy, you work for me. I am your Boss. I will provide for you."*

If I was working for God and doing what He called me to do, I could trust that He would help me to not only finish my book but also provide abundantly for me and my family. He would give me provision for this vision.

What is holding you back from completing the goal God has for you? Take time to evaluate and look for the windows of opportunity you have each day to work toward your goals. Is the early morning best for you or is it the afternoons when children are napping or at school? Or are you a night owl and find you are most productive after everyone else has gone to bed? Finding the time of day that best suits you and your energy level can help you to develop a rhythm and a flow to finish what God has called you to do. Take time to journal about the optimal time for you each day and what you hope to accomplish over these next 30 days. As you journal take time to listen, look at what God has already provided, and write down what He speaks to you.

Journal & Pray

The optimal time for me to work on my goals each day is . . .

____

____

____

Over these next 30 days, I pray God provides . . .

____

____

____

I plan to accomplish . . .

____

____

____

Day 15

Outside Your Comfort Zone

"Okay guys, I'll go first . . ."

I spoke the words and stepped into the murky waters of the lagoon on Marco Island in Florida. Being a Minnesota native and an adventurer, I jumped in and whispered a prayer along the way. Eric and the kids followed me as we sauntered across a sand bar through dark, waist-deep water, 100 yards or so to the other side. We held up all of our valuables including cell phones, car keys, beach chairs, and cooler so they wouldn't get wet. I prayed we wouldn't fall into a hole, get sucked into the mud, lose anything of value, or come face to face with a shark, alligator, or another antagonist in the brackish waters.

We were at Tiger Tail Beach. The reviews boasted this was one of the most beautiful beaches in Southwest

Florida. From the pictures we saw, we knew pristine white sands and gorgeous turquoise waters awaited us on the other side. And so we marched on. We couldn't see our final destination, but we moved forward in faith, knowing we would be rewarded with a great family time after our adventurous journey.

The trek across the bleak waters of the lagoon that day parallels the Christian walk. Oftentimes, God will ask you to step out in faith and it will not look pleasant or easy. Perhaps you can only see the dark waters and the dangers that lie beneath the surface. The unknown, the possibility of losing something of value, and overwhelming fear make you want to camp out in safety on the shore.

Living through the pandemic, economic instability, and inner-city riots of 2020 may have made you question if you ever wanted to leave the "safety bubble" of your home, let alone take a stand for your Christian faith in a politically charged world. Fear can paralyze your heart and make you just want to hide away.

During these times, God reminds me again, the safest place for me and my family is in the center of His will. He wants us to keep moving forward, to keep trusting Him, to keep doing what He has called us to do, and to take a stand for Him. Just like God helped us safely across the lagoon that day, we finished with a hike through the mangroves and then took in the most majestic ocean view imaginable. **Isaiah 26:7 (NLT/CE)** says "**But for those who are righteous, the path is not steep and rough. You are a God of justice, and you smooth out the road ahead of them.**"

As you trust God and take the next right step, He will make sure you are on solid ground, and He will smooth out the next step before you. If you place your hand in His and let Him lead you, you will not stumble on your way. If He leads you to it, He will bring you through it.

Take time to journal today and prayerfully pick one thing you can do to move forward. Take time to not only decide your next right step but also to ask God for His strategy in taking that step. Know you are not alone—He is walking with you every step of the way.

Journal & Pray

The next step I sense God leading me to take is . . .

___

___

___

The strategy I will use in taking this step is . . .

___

___

___

Day 16

Good-Bye Perfectionism

Oops, I did it again!

My cheeks burned and I was reeling as I left the green room at Steppenwolf Theater in Chicago. I wore an extremely expensive evening gown designed by Bella Freud, great-granddaughter of Sigmund Freud, and was preparing to model the dress at an annual black-tie affair.

Moments earlier, I approached two familiar-looking women and struck up a conversation. They were cordial and we exchanged pleasant banter. Then I commented as I looked at one of the women, "Haven't we worked together before? You look so familiar . . ."

My voice trailed off as a look of shock and then disdain spread across her face. *What did I say wrong? What did I do to offend her?* At that moment, one of the models called over to me and told me it was time to do our run.

My friend took in my flushed face and look of concern. "What did you say to her? She looks a little upset."

I repeated our conversation back to my model friend.

"Amy, don't you know who that is?" My friend mentioned her name. It was a famous actor from a well-known 90's sitcom. "You haven't worked with her. She is probably offended because you didn't recognize her. Be careful what you say next time, especially if you don't know who you are talking to."

I swallowed hard. I was only trying to be friendly. And now I was about to walk into the room to model the most expensive gown I ever wore in front of a wealth of influential and famous people. Growing up modestly in the woods of northern Minnesota with four brothers and a slew of animals did not prepare me for a job like this! I had to lean on God and trust Him to see me through.

Amy, shake it off. Pull it together. Forget it. You meant well. You can do this!

Zephaniah 3:17 (NKJV) says, "**The Lord your God in your midst, the Mighty One, will save; He will rejoice over you with gladness, He will quiet you with His love, He will rejoice over you with singing.**"

I made a quick decision at that moment. I could beat myself up over the mistake and let it affect my confidence, or I could let it go, flush it, and forgive myself. Thankfully, I opted for the latter. I didn't want to go out with a heavy heart and a conflicted face. I let go of my perfectionism and moved forward with grace.

We all make mistakes, every day. The beautiful thing is, we can learn from our mistakes. Often times failure is a better teacher than success. It's time to let go of the perfectionism that paralyzes us and move forward with grace, forgiveness, and humility.

As you journal today, take time to reflect on your experience yesterday. How did it feel to take the next right step? Take time to review your results, your emotional response, and then fill out the chart. As you learn to let go of paralyzing fear and perfectionism, you will be free to move forward one small step at a time. Remind yourself God loves you unconditionally, mistakes and all.

Journal & Pray

My reflections from yesterday on taking the next right step are . . .

____

____

____

Mistakes I have made in the past:	Lessons learned:
1. ____________.	1. ____________.
2. ____________.	2. ____________.
3. ____________.	3. ____________.

Paralysis that has held me back:	First small step:
1. ____________.	1. ____________.
2. ____________.	2. ____________.
3. ____________.	3. ____________.

Past victories/successes:	Resulting emotion/reflection:
1. ____________.	1. ____________.
2. ____________.	2. ____________.
3. ____________.	3. ____________.

Day 17

Extreme Make-Over

It's time to remodel.

If you walk downstairs with me, you no longer tread upon old, nasty carpet and maneuver around toys and piles of boxes that nearly reach the ceiling. We embarked on a seven-month project that included clearing out old furniture, files, boxes, toys, papers, cabinets, and tools. After everything was cleared out, including the tattered carpet, the restoration began. The only things that remained were the Scriptures we had written with markers on the cement walls when we did a prayer dedication over our home.

Similarly, when we let God into our lives, He clears out the old and begins to remodel and make things new. He doesn't want to just come into your living room and kitchen. He wants to move into the dark, cluttered closets, and the dingy, musty basement of your soul. He wants us to invite Him into the shame, the regret, and the hidden places in our hearts. He wants to come in and shine the light of His love and healing.

And He wants to rebuild our walls.

After we cleared out our basement and plans were formulated for the new living space, my husband and a couple of friends hauled in the wood and began framing out the new walls. **Isaiah 54:11–12 (NLT/CE)** says: **"O storm-battered city, troubled and desolate! I will rebuild you on a foundation of sapphires and make the walls of your houses from precious jewels. I will make your towers of sparkling rubies and your gates and walls of shining gems."** God wants to rebuild your life! It's important to remember that the temple in Jerusalem was rebuilt after the original one was destroyed and the Israelites had lived in exile for 70 years. It takes time. Embrace the process of rebuilding and know that God is working to make all things new, including you.

It all starts with inviting Him into the darkest places of your soul. Ask Him to come in, take the pain and shame and show you His perspective on your past. You can bring your deepest hurts to Him. Ask God to help you forgive those who have wounded you and then forgive yourself, too.

Let Him put up new walls and trust Him as He brings in the builders. Remodels can be dusty and messy, but rest assured, He will provide the right carpenters, plumbers, and flooring installers. He may bring those that are foreign to you to help hang drywall and install tile, but they are the right people for the job. Let people in again. Share your burdens with a trusted friend, mentor, therapist, or someone at your church. Ask for the right people to come alongside you as God does the extreme makeover in your heart and life. Know that the new process may disrupt things and create some disorder as God works to bring healing in your life, but when He is finished, you will stand in awe at all He has done.

Take time to journal today and pour out your heart to Him through your written words. He can be trusted with your deepest secrets. Ask God to bring the right builders into your life. Take time to revisit the people you listed from Day 9, the community God is leading you to in this season. Have you reached out yet? Know that He will be faithful to His promise, and He will help you to heal and rebuild as you take the next right step forward.

Journal & Pray

God, here are some of my deepest hurts and areas I need to experience Your healing . . .

____

____

The individual or group I plan to reach out to today for community is . . .

____

Here are some areas I need to remodel. . .
*Body (health improvements, fitness, new goals)

____

____

*Mind (training, research, reading, class/workshop)

____

____

*Spirit (serving others, confession of sin, prayer life, Christian therapy)

____

____

Day 18

Time Management

I woke up and the idea hit me, *30-30-30 . . .*

I implemented a new formula for time management and the plan stands for Speak-Write-Grow. Spend 30 minutes on each of these categories, each day of the workweek.

Writing, speaking, and growing my audience were constantly being squeezed out of my life. Dealing with all the effects of the pandemic, caring for children, homeschooling, managing our son's medical issues, and taking care of house and pets seemed to take up every minute of my day. Little time or energy remained to work on my personal or career goals. To stay productive, I decided to prioritize and establish some better strategies and time management in my day.

After talking to my husband and family, and communicating my frustration over not being able to work on my goals, they agreed to pitch in around the house and do more. I began to delegate chores, pets, and household responsibilities to my children and my husband. We began to work more as a team. I felt less overwhelmed, and I had more time freed up to implement my 30-30-30 plan.

I planned to continue to wake up early, spend time in Bible reading and prayer, and then get the kids started with school. Afterward, I walked our dog Blazer and cleaned up the dishes. I followed this up with exercise at home, usually a video or free class over YouTube, and then, a quick shower before I implemented the 30-30-30 plan.

I spend thirty minutes working on my writing. I either prepare a blog or work on my current book. I spend the next thirty minutes working on my speaking. I prepare my upcoming talks and rehearse them. Or I work on updating my speaking one sheet and put together a PowerPoint for one of my talks. And finally, the last 30 minutes are spent marketing the ministry online. Perhaps I spend time preparing for my Support Someone Saturday video broadcast on YouTube, or I spend time on social media responding to messages on Facebook and Instagram. Sometimes it means working on my upcoming monthly blog and newsletter.

Working on all these things, in small chunks of time,

motivates me and enables me to get something productive done. I don't feel as overwhelmed, which in the past has caused me to shut down and not do anything. As I accomplish small goals, it builds my confidence and my momentum. I am motivated to do more and see a project through to completion.

If you are a parent who is juggling many responsibilities like work, children's activities, homework, and household chores have you developed a strategy that works for you? God promised in **Deuteronomy 33:25 (The Living Bible)** that he would give you "**strength [to] match the length of your days.**" Take time to journal today and ask God to give you a time management plan that works best for you and your family in this new season.

Journal & Pray

The important things I would like to accomplish each day that keep getting pushed to the back burner are . . .

____

____

____

God, I believe You have a new time management plan for me. I plan to start implementing ____________________ each day.

The place I plan to work and the time frame I plan to do this daily are . . .

____

____

____

Day 19

Forgive & Be Free

On a cold, rainy, dreary day I sauntered out onto the walking path with my dog Blazer at my side.

While walking, my mind wandered to individuals who had recently hurt me and my family. It was one of those ongoing battles, where you have been hurt repeatedly by someone, and you try to figure out how to break free.

My first book just launched, and I was moving into a new career. Excitement and nerves intersected on this new path, yet I felt blessed to be fulfilling a life-long dream. I saw a vision of myself walking on this path, and suddenly in the vision, I saw a chain on my ankle which was attached to a large ball. It was like a ball and chain a prisoner wore back in the 17th and 18th centuries. At that moment, I realized the anger and unforgiveness I was harboring toward the ones who hurt me was keeping me chained down and holding me in place. I was stuck and could not move forward due to the weight and the entanglement.

I heard the still, small voice of the Lord, "Amy, if you don't forgive, you will be stuck in this place. This ball and chain you see laying off in the ditch, still attached to your ankle, will hold you back and keep you from moving forward on the path to fulfilling your destiny." Wow! Talk about a real eye-opener. The original pain I experienced was hard enough, but to think my bitterness and unforgiveness could rob me of my future blessing was just unbearable. I experienced enough loss already—I didn't want my future and my destiny to be stolen as well.

I knew what I had to do. I decided to forgive completely and let go as God called me to do. The people I needed to forgive had not said sorry or acknowledged the pain they had caused, but I was still called to forgive, nonetheless. Jesus' words as He hung on the cross echoed in my mind, **"Father, forgive them, for they know not what they do" (Luke 23:34, King James Version)**. These individuals were hurting, and they may not even realize the extent of the pain they had caused me and my family. Just as Jesus forgave those who crucified him, He was calling me to forgive those who wrongfully hurt me, too. Even if I didn't "feel" like I could forgive, and even though the pain was still raw and real, I put my trust in God that as I obeyed Him and forgave, He would deal with the individuals. I left it in His hands. My forgiveness toward these people would release the ball and chain from my leg and my life! I, in turn, would be free to move forward and to fulfill the destiny He had for me. **Matthew 5:44 (NKJV)** says, **"But I say to you, love your enemies, bless those who curse you, do good to those who hate you, and pray for those who spitefully use you and persecute you. . . "**

My peace of mind and my call to speak and write were more important than holding a grudge. I also didn't want bitterness to eat me up and destroy other important relationships in my life. I wanted to be free. Free to love and free to move forward. I began to pray a daily blessing over those who hurt me. Eventually, about a year after deciding to forgive and bless, I finally felt free. I no longer felt anger—only compassion. At times, the old hurts resurface and the people who hurt me will come to mind. Instead of rehearsing the old wounds in my mind, I say "Stop!" out loud. Then I choose to say out loud that I forgive the person who hurt me, and I pray a blessing over them and their loved ones. Since doing this, I am experiencing so much freedom and healing and am moving forward on the path toward my destiny.

I encourage you today to journal and as you write, choose to forgive, and pray a blessing over all those who hurt you. Watch how God intervenes to heal and to set you free.

Journal & Pray

God, I choose to forgive ______________________ for hurting me. I choose to release them from any obligation to pay back what was lost, stolen, or taken from me. I pray a blessing over ______________________ and all their loved ones, their marriage, their work, their finances, and over ______________________.

God, I know as I forgive and bless those who hurt me, You will heal my heart and set me free. Thank You for restoring all things and leading me on to the next step toward my destiny.

Day 20

Faith on the Battlefield

"Mom, maybe everything you and Dad have been through and everything God is having you teach us now, you will use to help other families in the future. It's like that verse we learned in AWANA (the weekly kids' Bible club, which stands for Approved Workmen Are Not Ashamed): "**Ask and it will be given to you, seek and you will find, knock and the door will be opened to you." Matthew 7:7 (NIV)**

Our then ten-year-old daughter, Arianna, spoke these words of wisdom to me as I sat reading with her before bed one night. She could sense my discouragement as we were facing family, finance, and health challenges. I sometimes questioned if we were on the right path and heading in the direction God had for us.

I decided to take my daughter's advice. Since I had been suffering from three bulging disks in my lower back and couldn't do a lot of physical activity, I set up a prayer "War" Room in our laundry room. I couldn't work out at the gym, vacuum, or even load the dishwasher, so I decided to ice my back in the laundry room and pray.

My friend Judi and I had recently gone to the Christian movie, *The War Room*, directed and produced by the Kendrick brothers. We both decided to roll up our sleeves, get on our knees, set up our War Rooms, and pray for our families and for our circumstances to change.

I put several prayer sheets up on the wall . . . one for Eric, one for Arianna, one for Ashton, and one for me. I also put up a sheet for Judi and her family. I was believing for breakthroughs in the areas of family, marriage, health, and finances.

Not long after I set up the War Room, my friend and former neighbor Carrie called. She said her brother-in-law, who was studying to be a priest at a seminary in Africa, called and asked Carrie and her husband Didier if there was a family they could pray for in America. Right away they thought of us.

"The Joob Family needs a new home!" Carrie exclaimed. She called and told me it was our turn for a new house as they recently moved out of our townhome community and into a spacious, single-family home. She let me know Didier's brother and the entire seminary would be fasting and praying one week for us. Every day they sent Scriptures from Psalms and the New Testament to encourage us. One day the Scriptures were for Eric and one day they were for me. The amazing thing is that during that same season of life Arianna and I were volunteering and running for clean drinking water in Africa through Team World Vision.

About two weeks after the time of prayer and fasting by the priests at the seminary, Eric and I were pre-approved to buy a new home. After feeling stuck and living in our townhouse for nearly 12 years, God flung the doors wide open a few months later to our new, beautiful, single-family home!

God really met me there. I wrote down Matthew 7:7–8 as Arianna had mentioned, and I put those verses up on the wall with others too. I continued to ask, seek, and knock, and God did not disappoint. I found an editor for my book and got onto the path of publishing. Within the year, we joined a new church, found a healthy community, and moved into our new home. I finally found healing and relief in my lower back as well.

Even though we suffered multiple setbacks as a family, God used that season in our lives to set us up for something greater. He was teaching me to press into His promises through prayer. I began intentionally interceding for my family, friends, church, and Christian ministries. In return, God took what seemed like several areas of setback to set us up for an amazing future. He faithfully ordered our steps and brought us to a new level of our destiny. We received healing, breakthrough, and provision in ways we could not imagine. He granted us favor and opened doors that exceeded our expectations. We were being thrust forward into our destiny as we prayed fervently and trusted Him.

Is there an area in your life that seems to be holding you back? Are you going around the same mountain again and again? Take time to journal today and ask God for a strategy for your breakthrough. Do you need to set up your own War Room? Once He gives you the solution, step out in faith, and don't look back. He will be faithful, and you won't be disappointed.

Journal & Pray

God, I feel like I have been going around the same mountain. I have been routinely held back in this area . . .

____

____

____

God, I pray You would show me the strategy for my breakthrough. As I pray today, the solution or next step that comes to mind is . . .

____

____

____

Day 21

Character Over Calling

"Amy, just take off your wedding ring, and I'm sure you'll get the job."

A friend was trying to help me land a bigger role on the movie set where we were filming in Chicago. As much as I wanted the part, I didn't want to compromise my values in exchange for it. A sense of unease came over me as I thought of taking off my wedding ring. My marriage was more important to me than landing any modeling or acting job.

After some thought, I responded, "If I have to take off my ring to get this job, then I don't want this job. My marriage is for life. These jobs will come and go. I am going to hang on to what is most important."

Maybe you are facing a similar circumstance where you are being tempted to compromise what you believe? As you take the next step toward your destiny, you may be presented with seemingly good opportunities or shortcuts along the way. I encourage you to pray about your next steps and the doors that open before you. If you don't have peace and if you have to compromise to move forward, look for a different path.

Pastor and Christian Author Mark Batterson says, "One of my recurrent prayers is this: Lord, don't let my gifts take me farther than my character can sustain me."[2]

As much as you want to achieve your goals, you don't want to do it at the cost of your character. Unfortunately, we have seen a lot of people fall from prominent positions in many aspects of our society. When we see them fall, we see the whole big mess. But I imagine it all started with one small compromise.

I did not take my wedding ring off that day. On occasion, before I went to a fitness print or commercial print job, I was asked to remove all jewelry. I always asked if I needed to take off my ring because I often played the part of a young mom or married person. I only took it off when necessary and kept it on when I did other jobs in the modeling industry. If it weren't for the strong support of my husband and the strength I found in our relationship and marriage, I don't even think I could have handled the pressures and the privileges I had during my modeling career.

Proverbs 10:9 says, **"Whoever walks in integrity**

walks securely, but whoever takes crooked paths will be found out."

I believe character counts. Eric and I were a part of teaching basic values through a campaign called "Character Counts" at the YMCA (Young Men's Christian Association) when we both worked there as college students. I believe character counts with God, and as you allow Him to develop your character, it will be the very thing that will sustain you as He brings you to a higher level of your destiny.

As you journal, take time to ask God to show you if there are any areas in your life where you have begun to compromise your values and your character. Ask for forgiveness and wisdom as you work to fulfill your goals. Make character and integrity your top priorities as you take the next right step today.

Journal & Pray

God, I pray will You reveal to me today if there are any areas of my life where I am compromising my character or values . . .

____

____

____

God, I pray You will give me wisdom and show me how I can make changes in my life. Moving forward, I plan to . . .

____

____

____

Day 22

Step into the New

I woke up early and exhaled deeply as I made my way to the couch with Bible and coffee cup in hand.

In a few short hours, I would be sitting at my first writing and publishing conference. I felt completely out of my element. I didn't have any experience and did not know how I could pull this one off without a lot of help from God. Not only was I going to attend this conference to learn more about writing and the publishing industry, but I also planned to pitch my manuscript and hoped to find a publisher for my first book.

I thought of all the years I worked in the modeling industry and the tradeshow industry. I had favor, experience, decent pay, friends, exciting work, and travel. I was at the top of my game. *Why am I making this transition now, at almost 50, onto a completely new career path? What am I thinking?*

I shoved the doubts down and asked God to calm my fears. I prayed for favor, wisdom, and for His Holy Spirit to make a way where there seemed to be no way. It felt like one of those moments where if God didn't show up it would be an epic fail.

Are you stepping out into something where you feel completely over your head? Is God leading you in a new direction or on a new career path? You can take comfort in **Psalm 37:23 (NLT), "The Lord directs the steps of the godly. He delights in every detail of their lives."** Even when you cannot clearly see the path ahead of you, and even though you may be blazing a new trail, you can rest assured that God is there with you and will lead every step of the way.

I began fasting and praying and asked some friends if they would do the same. Thankfully, with prayer warriors on my side as well as my friend, Debbie, and editor, Beth, coaching me, I knew I wasn't on the journey alone. I was also meeting my newly assigned mentor, Sue, at the conference.

Once I got there, I felt like I jumped into the deep end. A steep learning curve lay ahead of me, but at least I found the courage to attend. Taking the first step in a new direction is the hardest. But once you make that decision and take the leap, you start getting acclimated and meet people who steer you in the right direction.

Starting something new, moving in a new direction, or beginning a new line of work can be scary. But once you take the leap of faith in the direction God is leading you, you realize it is the most fulfilling and rewarding thing you could do. Often it's not as scary or as difficult as you feared it would be. You may even wish you took the leap sooner!

Take time to pray, journal, and listen for His still, small voice. In 1 Kings 19, you can read how Elijah the prophet is on the run from Jezebel and how he fears for his life. He is exhausted and wants to die. Despite this, God cares for his body and then his spirit. Elijah is able to hear the voice of God while he is hiding in a cave. Once Elijah finds a quiet place, he can hear from God. Perhaps you feel like you have been on the run or even hidden in a cave. As you wait, what do you hear God whispering to you? What new path is He leading you on, and what next right step do you need to take?

Journal & Pray

God, during this season of my life, I hear Your still, small voice directing me to . . .

____

____

____

God, I know I am not alone because You promised to never leave me. A key verse I plan to write down and stand on as I enter this new season is . . .

____

Day 23

Tell Me No Lies

A patch of slimy, hidden weeds tangled around my body as I swam across the lake in Madison, Wisconsin, and it felt like they were pulling me down.

Not only was I attempting one of my fastest swims, but I was also trying to qualify again for the USTS (United States Triathlon Series) Championship. I felt momentarily trapped and thought briefly, *I may drown.* I decided to dig deep, pray, and resist the lies of defeat, even as I worked feverishly to get untangled and swim forward on my quest to cross the lake.

Sometimes as we move toward the goals, dreams, and promises God has given us, we find ourselves fighting obstacles almost every step of the way. As soon as we cross over one hurdle, it seems like we are facing an even larger one.

As I charged forward on my bike during the second

trek of the race, I could feel pain searing across my lower back. I began to question how this race would pan out as my back seized up and competitors began to fly past me.

As I attempted to finish the run, the pain became greater. I prayed to finish strong and thought qualifying was out of my reach. I neared the end of the triathlon and limped over the finish line and was thankful to be done. My lower back injury came to a head during the race. I felt dejected and questioned my future in the sport. I thought my chances of qualifying for nationals were gone, but to my surprise, I finished in the top 15 and qualified after all.

It was a miracle I finished, let alone qualified for the championships. Unfortunately, due to the injury in my lower back, I was not able to attend or even train for triathlons for a season of my life. I felt grateful that God still allowed me to reach my goal of qualifying despite the pain in my body. God brought me vindication many years later as I signed up to do a small indoor triathlon at our local gym. It was my first race since that fateful day in Madison. I was completely surprised to find out after the race when they had tabulated the times for all the men and women, that I was the overall winner.

If you are weary and ready to throw in the towel on your dream today, I want to encourage you not to give up. Maybe you have tried numerous times to finish the book, launch the business, start your speaking career, or fulfill the dream God placed on your heart. You may be listening to lies like these . . . *You are too old. You are not smart enough. You have already tried and failed. You might as well just give up. This is never going to happen.*

I am here to tell you today that is not the truth. The enemy of our souls does not want you or me to succeed. He does not want you to fulfill your God-given destiny and he will do whatever it takes to discourage you, defeat you, and get you to give up on your dream. Don't let him win!

John 10:10 (NKJV) says, **"The thief does not come except to steal, and to kill, and to destroy. I have come that they may have life and that they may have it more abundantly."**

Take time to journal a prayer to God. First, confess where you have been discouraged and believed the lies. As we were reading yesterday, Elijah hit rock bottom as he ran from Jezebel. In I Kings 19:14 he laments to God that He is the only one left willing to serve God alone. However, God confronts him with the truth later in the chapter, as He declares that he has 7000 people in Israel that have not bowed their knee to Baal, the false god. As you journal your prayer, ask God to reveal to you where you have believed the lies. Then ask God to speak the truth, open the eyes of your understanding, and strengthen your faith. Remember, you are not alone on this faith journey. With God all things are possible! He will help you reach the next level of your destiny.

Journal & Pray

God, I confess the areas where I have been discouraged and believed lies . . .

____

____

____

God, I ask that You open the eyes of my understanding and speak the truth to me, especially in these areas . . .

____

____

____

Day 24

No More Excuses

After four months of sulking, eating ice cream, and creating excuses for why I couldn't work on my manuscript, I finally gave in.

I sat back down at the computer and opened the file. The latest review from my editor made me question my capabilities of finishing the memoir on my own. After lots of prayer and encouragement from friends and family, I determined to try again.

I heeded my editor's advice, read and re-read the two books she suggested, and prayed God would give me wisdom and understanding on how to make the necessary changes. Fear and insecurity clouded my mind at times, and I confronted the lie I was incapable of finishing the book. Sitting back down and opening the file that day was a breakthrough. Slowly, I read through my manuscript again and whispered prayers along the way that God would enable me to complete what He called me to do.

I reached the point where the pain of staying the same had become greater than the pain of change. Years earlier Eric's dad, Pastor Fred, had taught us this principle and it applied to me now. (It's the same principle taught by Dr. Henry Cloud and Dr. John Townsend in the book *Boundaries,* Zondervan, 1992.*)* Yes, it seemed nearly impossible at times to figure out the next right step on this journey. And one of the biggest obstacles to overcome was my own unbelief. I was determined to face and overcome my feelings of inadequacy and embrace the pain of change.

It's easy to find excuses and even legitimate reasons why you cannot do something or complete what is required of you. Perhaps you can even find sympathetic friends and family members who will stand with you. But at the end of the day, you will not be fulfilled or have the self-satisfaction that you overcame all the obstacles and finished the task you set out to do.

And not only will you feel disappointed in yourself, but you will also have the sense you let God down. If He truly calls you to do something, He will help you to complete it. He will bring the right people onto your path who will teach you, mentor you, and counsel you. And He will give you the wisdom, grace, and strength you need to finish what He has called you to do. **Philippians 4:13 (NKJV)** says, **"I can do all things through Christ who strengthens me."**

So during those moments when you feel completely overwhelmed and unqualified for the job, take time to pray and invite others to pray with you. Ask Him for the wisdom and strength you need. Ask Him to bring key people into your life who will support you and help you. He will be faithful.

We just need to do our part. We need to pray and then move forward in the direction He is leading us. We need to put down doubt and excuses and pick up our faith and courage once again. Just take the next baby step forward. Today is the day to get up and try again.

Take time to pray and journal today about the different reasons you have quit moving forward. Pray that He would show you what may be holding you back. Pray for a fresh revelation from Him and a key strategy you can implement to move forward again.

Journal & Pray

Source of Pain:	Strategy:	Benefit:
Avoiding exercise/ Gaining weight	Run or do workout video before breakfast	Better mood/energy to handle kids/ homeschooling
Overwhelmed by housework/not working on book	Have kids help do laundry and chores	Not giving in to kids' complaining teaches them independence
______________	______________	______________
______________	______________	______________
______________	______________	______________
______________	______________	______________
______________	______________	______________
______________	______________	______________
______________	______________	______________
______________	______________	______________
______________	______________	______________

Day 25

Speak Life

My family is made up of driven, type-A people. We all have strong opinions and convictions and arguments to back them up. At the dinner table, we often interrupt and talk over one another as we passionately share what we believe. It's something we have become more aware of and are working on as a family.

As a mom, I have prayed about how to corral the chaos in our home and in our spirited conversations. During prayer, God started to impress upon me the importance of speaking words of life over my husband and my children. **Proverbs 18:21 (NKJV)** says, "**Death and life are in the power of the tongue, and those who love it will eat its fruit.**" I began to see how our words either build each other up and make our family stronger, or how they tear us down. The revelation of the power and impact of our words became very clear.

I talked to Eric, and we started to be intentional about building unity in our family once again. We reimplemented the weekly family meetings we started when the children were young. We went through a season where we wrote letters of encouragement to one another, and we would call out each other's strengths. We got out the God Box, dusted it off, and opened it once again. We each wrote down two things on two slips of paper of how we see God at work and how He is answering our prayers and showing Himself faithful to our family.

Other times, we go around the table and do the sixty-second boost. Each person, for sixty seconds, gives a boost of verbal affirmation and encouragement to the one in the "hot seat." During broken times and challenging seasons, we give ourselves permission to share the hard, painful emotions we feel. We give each family member ten minutes to share everything that is burdening them, including the most difficult topics that seem off-limits, and the rest of us work to just listen and not interrupt the one who is sharing their heart.

God is giving us the ability in our families to help one another heal. As a parent, you can begin to speak life and call out greatness in your children, teens, or young adults. As a wife or husband, you can affirm the plan and purpose of God over your spouse's life. In prayer, you can journal or even decree out loud the promises of God over yourself, your spouse, your children, your family, and your future.

I would encourage you to find creative ways to speak life over yourself and your family today. Perhaps, you can put up a Bible verse that speaks to your situation on your bathroom mirror or kitchen window. You can also write your children letters, or give your spouse an encouraging card or text. You can be creative around the holidays and put up hearts or pumpkins on the bedroom doors, one for each day of the month, with an affirmation about your loved one. Putting up positive words of encouragement and promises from the Bible can give you and your family the hope and boost of faith you all need. As you intentionally speak words of life, I believe you will see much fruit.

Take time to journal today. Where have you been speaking doubt, negativity, or death over your situation? Ask God to show you and ask Him to help you speak positive words over yourself, your loved ones, and your situation today.

Journal & Pray

God, I confess I have been speaking doubt, unbelief, and negative words in this area over myself and other people . . .

____

____

____

Affirmation Goal For Today

Person to Bless	Means to Share	Message
My husband	Text	Thank him for going on date with me
My mom & dad	Card/Gift Card	Encourage them in a hard season
1. __________	__________	__________
2. __________	__________	__________
3. __________	__________	__________

Day 26

Do It Afraid[3]

I stepped onto the stage adorned in my long, sleek, beaded dress and tall acrylic slippers.

Unbeknown to others, I was carrying something extremely precious with me. I recently found out I was two months pregnant, and only Eric knew.

A few years earlier, I wore this same ensemble in the Mrs. Illinois Pageant. I walked onto the stage for the first time in high heels and felt nervous at the newness of everything. This time I felt a sense of vulnerability as I carried my first baby in my womb.

My job for the evening was to be "Vanna" on stage and simply hand out awards for a big corporation. As I mounted the stage, I prayed for strength, to not feel nauseous, and for the pregnancy to go unnoticed. It is strange to be in the beauty business where you are hired based on your looks and figure and you have to hide things like pregnancy. I whispered prayers all would go well.

Everything started smoothly with the first couple of award winners. Then noticeably, the crowd seemed to get rowdier as they consumed food and plentiful drinks. The noise level in the room rose and an unhinged party atmosphere permeated the air. When the next award recipient took the stage, something told me I was about to earn my pay.

"I want to kiss the pretty girl on stage!" He shouted obnoxiously as he locked eyes with me and barged up the steps and onto the platform.

The crowd started chanting, "Kiss her! Kiss her!" I never felt more publicly humiliated and afraid than I did at that moment.

I immediately prayed for God to intervene. **John 14:27** says, **"Peace I leave with you, my peace I give you . . . Do not let your hearts be troubled and do not be afraid."** I prayed for wisdom and that the presenter would speak up and stop the nonsense. I scanned the room for a sympathetic woman to step in. I only had a few moments to figure out what to do and realized I may need to handle things myself, with God's help.

As the tipsy man approached me to receive his award, the presenter attempted to quiet the crowd. I steadied my legs, squared my high heels firmly on the platform, and prepared to defend myself and my baby I was carrying inside. My heart felt like it was beating outside of my chest. I squinted my eyes and glared with a scowl as I held out the trophy far from my body. I shook my head "no" and shot daggers at him through my eyes. He read my body language and his reckless behavior started to fade.

"I was just joking—I, I wouldn't do that," he stuttered as he grabbed his award and walked off stage, smirking even as he spoke the words.

Thankfully it was over soon, and I couldn't wait to leave. As I said goodbye, my client gave me my paycheck plus a very nice tip. I felt relief wash over me and thanked God for His protection that night on stage. I faced my fear of working with a hidden pregnancy, and God was faithful to keep me and Arianna safe. I was blessed to find work through about seven months of my pregnancy due to caring and compassionate clients and agents in the business.

Take time to journal about how God is asking you to step outside your comfort zone and "do it afraid." How have you stepped out in the past and how has God shown up for you? Write a prayer and ask Him to give you the courage to take the next right step in faith once again.

Journal & Pray

God, I acknowledge this fear to You that has held me back . . .

____

____

____

I know You are asking me to push past this fear. Please give me the courage to take a step of faith by . . .

____

____

____

Thank You, God, for showing up in the past, helping me to overcome this fear and to accomplish . . .

____

____

____

Day 27

Pray For Others

I sat in my "War Room," a.k.a. the laundry room, yet again, and poured out my heart to God.

Back on Day 20, I talked about *The War Room,* a movie directed by the Kendrick brothers. The premise of the movie is about a married couple who outwardly seem to have it all, but inwardly their marriage is crumbling. The wife sets up a War Room and presses into God through prayer for a miracle to save their family.

Our family went through so much transition during that year. I found an editor and was focusing on completing my first book. I was nursing three bulging disks and praying for relief from the pain. The rest and ice time on my back served a dual purpose as I prayed.

I interceded for my family, prayed for my husband to be blessed and promoted in his work, and pressed into God's promises as I prayed for my book to be finished.

I prayed for abundant financial provision. I prayed for Team World Vision and clean drinking water for those living in underdeveloped communities around the world.

I also fasted and prayed with the City Director at Refuge for Women, that God would provide the first safe home in Illinois for women who desired to leave sex trafficking and start fresh in life. I heard a pastor say, "If you take care of what is on the heart of God, He will take care of what is on your heart." As I prayed for these ministries, I noticed He began to work behind the scenes on our needs as well.

A couple of months into this season of prayer, our then six-year-old son, Ashton, scampered up to me and asked, "Mom, when are we going to get a house? God said it's time." *The faith of a child.* We longed for a single-family home for years while living in a small townhome. Life circumstances, medical bills, and difficulties in business had kept us in our current place. When Ashton mentioned this again with such confidence, both Eric and I started to pray and seek God.

About a month after Ashton's exuberant statement of faith, Eric and I met with our realtor. He told us we could rent our townhome for the exact price of our monthly mortgage payment, and within three days we received approval from the mortgage lender. We found our home about three months later and closed by the end of the school year. Right around the same time, Refuge for Women received financing and closed on their first safe home in Illinois.

As I took time for intentional prayer and focused on praying for others, God, in turn not only met but exceeded our expectations. **Ephesians 3:20 (NLT/CE)** says, "**Now glory be to God! By his mighty power at work within us, he is able to accomplish infinitely more than we would ever dare to ask or hope.**" Take time to journal and ask God if there is someone He wants you to pray for too. As you focus on Him and praying for others, He will take care of you and bless you in ways you can't even imagine. He will be faithful to guide you to your next right step.

Journal & Pray

God, I sense You are asking me to pray for ___________.
Today, I pray that You would bless . . .

____

____

____

God, even as I ponder my next right step, show me how I can encourage or help this person/people to take their next right step today . . .

____

____

____

Day 28

Rest Awhile

If you are working like crazy and barely coming up for a breath, it may be time to take a break and give yourself permission to rest.

As a type-A personality, I am familiar with the drive to push yourself to work until you are weary. You may have a project in the works or a looming deadline to meet. As soon as you reach that deadline you immediately start the next project. Can you relate? Maybe you have a performance-based, high-achievement personality type too.

Especially as I get older, I realize the importance of rest. If I do not take a break, I will end up breaking down. I may burn out, get sick, or blow up at those I love the most. Slowly, I am learning as God is showing me a smarter, more strategic way. When I feel like I am running on empty, I plan to take time off to re-charge so that I have the stamina to complete the goals I set out to do. God prompted both me and my husband, Eric, to intentionally take a weekly sabbath, one day off a week to truly rest and recharge.

Honestly, as I was nearing the deadline for my first book to be published, I had an emotional meltdown. We were traveling home from the Christmas holidays in Minnesota and dodging a snowstorm. I felt angry at my husband because I didn't agree with how he was handling the kids. It triggered past issues in me. We were all stressed and frazzled, and I blew up in anger at my entire family as we stopped for lunch that day. I spewed my stress and frustration all over them. I felt exhausted and overwhelmed about everything and needed a sanity break.

Ever since the colossal meltdown and regret that ensued, I have been working to change my perspective on work and rest. Instead of being in the driver's seat and determining the speed, duration, and direction of the vehicle, I have decided to hop into the passenger seat. I am letting Jesus take the wheel and begin to direct my work, rest, and life for me. It's refreshing and enlightening to let Him determine when it is time to work and when it is time to take a pit stop to rest. I am also trusting He will provide enough to cover my bills as the reality becomes clear that I don't need to work non-stop.

One of my favorite verses is **Matthew 11:28–30 (NLT)**, in which Jesus says, "**Come to me, all of you who are weary and carry heavy burdens, and I will give you rest. Take my yoke upon you. Let me teach you, because I am humble and gentle at heart, and you will find rest for your souls. For my yoke is easy to bear, and the burden I give you is light.**"

As you pray, take time to evaluate your current work/life balance. Are you resting enough? Are you trusting God with your work, your business, and your life? If not, ask God to show you areas where you can make changes and strategies you can implement to create more time for rest.

Journal & Pray

God, show me any areas in my work, business, or life where I am out of balance . . .

____

____

____

As I pray about making changes, please show me strategies and give me a game plan for how I can add consistent rest times in my schedule . . .

____

____

____

Day 29

Believe in Your Destiny

"And the winner of the 2019 Write-To-Publish Best New Writer is . . . Amy Joob for *Model Behavior: Make Your Career Path Your Calling!*"

I jumped out of my seat as tears began to flow down my cheeks. A wave of awe, disbelief, and excitement washed over me. *Is this actually happening to me?* I invested over seven years and a handsome sum of money to write and publish my first book and it felt like all the late nights and sacrifices had paid off! As I approached the front of the room, I felt like God was validating His call on my life to write. I gave Lin Johnson, the conference director, a big hug as I tearfully accepted my award.

When I got home, I shared the good news with my family. Our son Ashton, who was 10 years old at the time, said to me, "Mom, you should put this award up on the wall, and right next to it you should put a sign that says, 'What doesn't kill you makes you stronger.'" He gave an accurate synopsis of writing my first book, even quoting the hit song "Stronger" by artist Kelly Clarkson.

Later, I reflected on my writing journey and my college years. I was determined to get all A's in class and as a conscientious student, it seemed like a goal within my reach. However, my English literature professor did not feel the same way. I thought writing was one of my stronger skills, yet for some reason, I couldn't seem to earn his approval and I couldn't get an A on any of my papers. I walked into his office one day, sat across the desk from him, and asked him how I could improve my grade.

He looked at me with a condescending smirk on his face and said, "There is nothing you can do to bring up your grade. I don't care what you do, you will not get an A in this class. The highest grade you will earn is a B. I have nothing further to discuss with you."

I swallowed the lump in my throat and tried not to cry. I knew there was no use in arguing or trying to reason with him. For whatever reason, my professor had made up his mind that I only deserved a B in his class.

The fear, insecurity, and doubt brought on by that conversation with my professor put a dark shadow over me and made me completely question my ability to write. If I was an A student overall and one of the top students in criminal justice, and yet I couldn't get an A in English literature, was I even qualified to write?

However, my English literature professor and his opinion on my writing were not the final word. God always has the final word. God won't change His mind or take away the call on your life, even if others don't always validate you or your talents. **Proverbs 18:16 (NKJV)** says, **"A man's gift makes room for him, and brings him before great men."** No matter what you have done or what others say, your gift and your calling stand firm with Him. Keep moving forward as He leads and trust Him to make a way where there seems to be no way.

I want to encourage you that God will have the final say. As you journal today, forgive those who have spoken against you, downplayed your gifts, or squashed your dreams. Pray a blessing over those people. Shake it off and keep moving forward. God is the author and finisher of your faith, and He will determine how your story will end. God will use every part of your story for His glory!

Journal & Pray

God, I want to forgive ______________________________ for. . .

____

____

____

Even though hurtful things were spoken over me, it is not the final word on the giftings You have given me. I choose to forgive and pray this blessing . . .

____

____

____

God, show me again today Your vision for how You want me to use my gifts to bless those around me . . .

____

____

____

Day 30

Sudden Blessings

Since the Noonan Syndrome diagnosis in 2017, Ashton routinely goes to see 10 different specialists and therapists. It took two years of doctors, tests, and specialists to get to the bottom of all the issues with his health. Even with insurance, our medical bills were mounting. We were trying to figure out how to keep Ashton on his daily growth hormone medication, which is extremely expensive and which he needs to take until he is at least 16 years old.

One overcast day in March of 2018, as I was driving down our street after doing some volunteer work for a non-profit, my heart felt heavy over the circumstances with Ashton's health, the denial we received from the third insurance appeal, and all the bills surrounding his care. I whispered a prayer, "I trust you, Jesus," and my phone instantly rang. My friend Heather was on the other end of the line.

"Amy, I have been praying for you guys. Will you please let me start a Go Fund Me for Ashton?" Tears rolled down my cheeks as I thanked God for answering my prayer at the very moment I cried out to Him. He knew what we needed and when we needed it most.

The Go Fund Me created by Heather helped us erase our medical debt and enabled us to go to the MAGIC Foundation Convention for the first time as a family in the summer of 2018. When your child is diagnosed with a rare disorder, you discover that answers, as well as support and understanding, can be hard to find. The MAGIC Foundation provides resources, education, and networking opportunities for children and families that are affected by any type of growth hormone disorder. From my experience working at the MAGIC Foundation Convention as an independent contractor during my modeling career, I knew they were the support Ashton and our family needed.

About six months later, after an exhausting holiday season and lots of hard work, my first book, *Model Behavior: Make Your Career Path Your Calling,* was published on January 28, 2019. The very same week in January, my husband launched his new business, AV3 Productions. We were seeing life-long dreams come true at the very same time! And the icing on the cake was winning "Best New Writer" at the Write-To-Publish Conference later in 2019.

In July of 2019, our family flew on an airplane for the first time together to Florida. Family friends blessed us by allowing us to stay at their home in Naples. The kids swam in the ocean for the first time, and my friend Simi helped me host a book signing in Bradenton.

In November, our son Ashton was chosen by Novo Nordisk to be a patient/model for Nordotropin (growth hormone medication) and featured in Europe. We were flown out to New Jersey and spent several days there and in New York, sightseeing and working at the photo-shoot. God poured out His goodness and it seemed to erase the sadness and the suffering we had experienced the previous few years.

God works through "suddenlies." We were in a season of seeing several lifelong dreams suddenly come true at the very same time. I know if He can do it for me and my family, He can do it for you and yours!

Right now, you may be trudging through a long, difficult season. You may feel like you are ready to give up. Don't stop now. I believe your suddenly and your breakthrough are closer than you think!

Even if you are going through a hard time, do not quit. Keep the faith and keep persevering. It may seem like you will never get unstuck, but your breakthrough is on the way. Keep trusting Him and keep trusting His perfect timing. Remember it is always darkest before the dawn.

Suddenly, God, your light floods my path,
God drives out the darkness.
I smash the bands of marauders,
I vault the high fences.
What a God! His road
Stretches straight and smooth.
Every God-direction is road-tested.
Everyone who runs toward him
Makes it.[4]

2 Samuel 22:29-31 (The Message)

As you journal today, reflect on God's faithfulness in your life. How has He answered prayers and shown His faithfulness before? What miracles are you still believing for? Take time to thank Him for His goodness and continue to trust Him for His perfect provision. Have hope and continue to believe He will bring good things to pass in your life in His perfect way and in His perfect time.

Journal & Pray

God, thank You for Your faithfulness in my life. I'm thankful and blessed by how You have answered these prayers . . .

___

___

___

God, I know You've answered my prayers before, and You will do it again. Thank You for hearing and answering me. I am believing You for clarity, direction, and breakthrough in these areas . . .

___

___

___

Day 31

The Secret Place

People sometimes ask, "what is your secret?"

How have I been able to handle all the adversity, challenges, pressure, and life-altering circumstances that have come my way? I'll admit, I cannot do it on my own or in my own strength. My secret is Jesus and spending time in the secret place with Him. I wake up early in the morning and find a hot cup of coffee and a quiet place where I can be alone with Him. I pour out my heart, let down my guard, and just get real. Sometimes I write in my journal and other times I talk to Jesus like He is sitting there next to me. I know He won't judge me, and I can cry, weep, vent, question, and lay down my cares.

The secret place is a place of intimacy between you and Jesus. A place to thank Him, affirm your trust in Him, and present petitions and heartaches too. For me, going to the secret place is making time and creating space to be still and hear His voice.

To get to the secret place, you have to be intentional. Clear your schedule and guard against distractions. The secret place is powerful because it is a War Room where strategies are given and plans are made to defeat the enemy. It's the place where God can exhort and commission you for your next assignment. It is a place of great comfort when you have gone through loss and grief that you cannot even express in words.

The secret place is like a birthing chamber where your dreams come to fruition and a hospital room where your heart and soul are healed. It is so important for every believer, and for me, I cannot thrive without spending time there. Living the Christian life without being in the secret place with Jesus is like trying to drive your car across many states but never stopping to put gas into your vehicle. In order to move forward, have the energy to carry on, and gain insight to find your next right step, you have to spend time with Him in the secret place.

And not only will you find strength and protection there, but you will also find rewards that come from Him. You will have more peace, patience, and wisdom in dealing with people and circumstances. You will find God begins to open doors you could never imagine. He will reward you with opportunities and divine appointments.

He is looking for those with hearts completely surrendered to Him. **Psalm 91:1 (NKJV)** states, **"He who dwells in the secret place of the Most High shall abide under the shadow of the Almighty"** and in **Hebrews 11:6 (NKJV)** it says, **"He is a rewarder of those who diligently seek Him."** He is looking for those He can trust to carry out His plans and bring His love to our hurting world.

During the pandemic, we went through a couple of challenging months with major dental and health issues in our family. We were trying to figure out how to keep my husband's business afloat since he did live events and how we could earn money during the shutdown. I spent much time in prayer in the secret place. During that time, new dreams were being birthed within me. God showed me the importance of completing this prayer journal and gave me the idea to launch the video podcast, *Support Someone Saturday.* My desire is to get the word out about charities, non-profits, and ministries doing good to help others even during major crises happening in our country and world. I launched the podcast and my YouTube channel, *Esther and Mordecai Generation,* as a result of this time in prayer.

Also during this season, I was awarded a scholarship

to be coached by an author and speaker who is much further along than me and we received surprising financial provision in the form of a tax refund, which we hadn't received in years! I believe as you and I spend quality time with Jesus in the secret place, He will answer our prayers, give us divine strategies, and often exceed our expectations. He will give us not only the next right steps, but He will also provide provision for the vision.

I encourage you today to journal and talk to Jesus about everything. Let Him know your requests and pour out your heart to Him. Listen as He shares His heart with you and shows you the next right step that He has for you. Make time for Him in the secret place each day.

Journal & Pray

God, thank You that I can know You intimately through Your son Jesus Christ. As I come into the secret place with You today, I want to thank You for . . .

____

____

____

God, I want to present these petitions to You today . . .

____

____

____

I pray that You would show me the next right steps and Your divine strategy to handle what I am facing today . . .

____

____

____

Day 32

Ask For Helpers

As I rode the tidal wave of my first book being published and launched, about three months in, I wondered how I could keep the momentum to promote and market my book all year.

I felt exhausted from juggling family, work, travel, book promotion, and Eric's new business. I did what I normally do in moments like these - I called on God. His phone number is **Jeremiah 33:3 (NKJV): "Call to me, and I will answer you, and show you great and mighty things, which you do not know."** I asked God for helpers and key people who could assist me and my family members in areas we needed it the most.

Within a month, I was sitting down at my dining room table with our good friend and former babysitter, Laura. Not only is she a college grad and an amazing artist, but she also has her own online business and is knowledgeable about social media and marketing. Laura was an answer to my prayers! Her youthful energy, social media skills, and business/marketing savvy were the perfect match for me. And to top it off, Laura is a committed Christian who loves God and serves at church in the youth group. Laura became my virtual assistant.

I took her up on her offer to help me grow my social media and expand my marketing online. Laura kept me organized and on task and helped me create my monthly newsletter, email blogs, graphics for *Support Someone Saturday*, and my new website. I am so thankful for her timely support, creativity, and expertise in a season where I felt like I was drowning.

If you feel like you are lacking skills or wisdom in an area and you feel stuck, I encourage you to pray and ask God for help. I encourage you to pray for Him to align you with the right people.

God is so faithful! He knows the end from the beginning, and He is the one calling you and creating you for an amazing destiny. None of us has all the skills individually to complete the goals He has given us. He has called us to partnership, relationships, and community. I know He has the perfect person lined up to help you even now. **1 Corinthians 3:9** says, **"For we are co-workers in God's service; you are God's field, God's building."** God is indeed working in and through your life, and

He will be faithful to provide the right helpers to come alongside you.

As you journal today, write about the areas where you have struggled and where you are coming up short. Let Him know the desires of your heart and the areas where you need some support and guidance. I believe God will bring the right people into your life and give you wisdom regarding who to partner with in this next season of life. I believe that not only do you need others to help you achieve your dream and destiny, but others need your help and expertise too.

Journal & Pray

God, I feel overwhelmed and am struggling in these areas . . .

___

___

___

God, I could use some support and guidance in these areas. Give me wisdom, clarity, and insight into who I can partner with in this season. Please bring the right people into my life and show me now if there is someone I should reach out to . . .

___

___

___

Day 33

Celebrate Small Beginnings

When you are starting something new, it can feel awkward.

You may be stepping into a new role in business, online, or in ministry. You may feel like you don't measure up to more seasoned professionals or others around you and you may question your capabilities.

I know the feeling. I have walked through this season of life a few times. Starting a new career or a new venture is a lot like launching a kite off the ground. You need the right amount of wind, and you have to run fast enough to get your kite up into the air and flying on its own. It's important to keep focused and not give up, even when things feel uncomfortable and strange because your persistence will get the kite up into the air and your determination will keep you sailing along.

When I went to my first publishing conference, I felt like I just jumped into the deep end of the pool. Not only had I never been to a writing or publishing conference, but the only people I knew in the industry were my friend who is a Christian public relations agent, and the editor I worked with on my manuscript. Thankfully, those who put on the conference provided a lot of materials beforehand to help us prepare for pitching our manuscripts to the editors there. I think the more you study, learn, and prepare in the beginning, the more comfortable you will begin to feel. It's never easy to start over or learn something brand new, but if you are patient with yourself and if you are teachable, you are well on your way to launching your kite into the new.

Often during the process of publishing my first book, and as I began to market *Model Behavior* at events around the country, I reminded myself to not despise small beginnings. Even though I may have experienced a smaller turnout at an event than I anticipated, or I only sold two copies of my book that day, I decided to keep a positive attitude and remember that I was still moving forward. I was building up a following on social media and through an email list and getting my name and the title of my book out there. At times like this, you need to remind yourself persistence will pay off!

Book publishing and marketing is not for the faint

of heart, especially for first-time authors. It is a journey and a learning experience. And it's important to keep in mind that even the bigtime, best-selling authors were once at the beginning too. **Zechariah 4:10 (NLT/CE)** says, **"Do not despise these small beginnings, for the Lord rejoices to see the work begin."** God is with you, and He will open doors for you as you faithfully obey Him. So keep persevering, keep moving forward, and trust Him.

As you journal today, take time to share with God your doubts and your challenges. What new thing is He asking you to do? If you are in the beginning stages of a new career, project, or job, ask Him to give you motivation and wisdom as you keep moving forward. Ask Him to show you things from His perspective.

Journal & Pray

God, today I ask that You take these doubts, concerns, and challenges . . .

____

____

____

God, please show me things from Your perspective. I know You see the end from the beginning. Show me Your perspective on my new endeavor and my current situation. God, my hope and desire is that You will . . .

____

____

____

Day 34

Hard Things First

A continual pile of mail and papers sit in my house, usually on my desk, on the kitchen counter, or an extra chair in the dining room.

I can't stand sorting through the mail and filing papers. Add to that my habit of note-taking and list-making, and you will find pieces of paper floating around my house everywhere. I do not enjoy the simple yet menial task of sorting through bills, mail, receipts, flyers, and children's school papers. Therefore, I regularly have a mounting pile of paperwork in my house. One time in desperation I paid our son to help make the pile of papers disappear. I need motivation and accountability to finish the hard tasks. Ashton's young legs running up and down the stairs to put papers in their proper places was well worth the money spent.

What is your least favorite task or job to do? My

suggestion is to do it first thing in the morning after you have a cup of coffee and your quiet time with God. I make myself get up early, fighting the urge to stay in bed, snuggling my husband. I soak up the solitude and enjoy a cup of steamy brew as I journal, read my Bible, and pray. Next, I put on my workout clothes and either walk the dog or head to the gym.

After my morning routine, I face the most dreaded task of the day. Sometimes, it may be sorting papers or paying bills. Other times it is a phone call or email I have been putting off. Often, I have to call our insurance, schedule a doctor or therapist visit, or order my son's medicine. I put my phone on speaker while on hold to do laundry or dishes while I'm waiting for the person to pick up on the other end.

What are you putting off? What is necessary but difficult for you to do? May I suggest setting your alarm, waking up early, and making the dreaded task one of the first things you do? It may not be fun, but you will feel a huge burden lift when it's done. You will gain momentum as everything else moves downhill during your day. **Proverbs 21:5 (NLT)** says, **"Good planning and hard work lead to prosperity, but hasty shortcuts lead to poverty."** As you journal today, ask God for wisdom and motivation to start a new routine and for help tackling the hard things first each day.

Journal & Pray

God, I know am putting these things off and procrastinating in this area . . .

My plan for this week is to do one hard task, first thing each day.

Day:	Task:	Check if completed:
(Example)	Fill out new passport app	✓
(Example)	Find formatter for my book	✓
Monday		
Tuesday		
Wednesday		
Thursday		
Friday		
Saturday		

Day 35

Right Alignment

Have you ever been driving and suddenly you feel the car "pull" to one side of the road? Perhaps you take your hands slightly off the wheel and notice the car veers out of the lane. Most likely, the car is out of alignment. You need to take it in to have the tires rotated and the wheels aligned so you can travel safely on the road again.

As you step into a new assignment, you may realize that you are not heading in the right direction with your current set of wheels. You need key people to help you walk through the new door God has for you. I often pray that He would send me the right gatekeepers to enable me to walk through the new door of my destiny. It doesn't mean you have to leave everyone in your life behind. It just means there are other like-minded people out there, heading in the same direction you are, and they can help facilitate your move. Those people may already be established in the place you are heading, or they have the tools to help you gain access to the door. Perhaps they are also walking through the same door as you.

When God brings the right alignment, you discover you instantly click with these new people as you share your passion and your vision with them. We all need the right people to partner with to be successful and fruitful in the new assignment God has called us to.

Revelation 3:8 says, "**I know your deeds. See, I have placed before you an open door that no one can shut. I know that you have little strength, yet you have kept my word and not denied My name.**"

I encourage you to seek out the right alignment and pray God brings the right people onto your path. I also pray God removes anyone that may be hindering my progress or holding me back from the new place God is bringing me. As I am praying for others to support me, I realize I may be a gatekeeper or a catalyst for change in someone else's life as well. I am open as God leads me to help those I can too.

Today, journal and pray about the right alignment in your life. Is God nudging you to reach out to someone? Is He prompting you to find a life coach, mentor, counselor, or another professional? Is He leading you to get into a new network or go back to college? I would encourage you to take time to listen for His voice and think back to recent conversations or invites you have received from others. In what new direction is God leading you? Ask God to reveal the right connections and the new doors He wants you to walk through. As you take steps of faith, I believe you will reach a new level of your destiny.

Journal & Pray

God, I pray You would show me who You would like me to partner with in this season. I sense You are leading me to . . .

____

____

____

God, please show me if You want me to follow up or pursue any new leads? Some recent conversations and invites I've received are . . .

____

____

____

Day 36

Implement God's Strategies

Living through the pandemic of 2020 felt like blazing a trail in the dark through a desolate, dense forest.

This season of life was unparalleled; lockdowns and sickness across the globe were incomparable and unmatched by any other period in history. According to Webster's dictionary, unparalleled means "having no equal or match; unique in kind or quality."[5] None of us could have imagined going down this road. We all scrambled to figure out how to process the pandemic and life events, manage the shifts in work and school, and somehow keep moving forward despite it all.

We learned to juggle online events, remote learning, homeschooling, Zoom meetings, virtual church, and working from home. We started ordering groceries and household products online and meals to go from Uber

Eats and Door Dash. With advancements in technology, we could now see who was buzzing at our door even when we were away, through devices like Ring. And all the while, the way we did work, ministry, and life changed too. We were all stretched, propelled out of our comfort zones, and thrust into a whole new system of communicating, interacting with others, and carrying out our daily lives. Through all this we learned to become more flexible, adaptable, and resilient.

Maybe you are adjusting to a new job or learning a new career, or you may be navigating how to bring your current job, ministry, or business up to speed and online. Never before have we had such a great need for wisdom, grace, knowledge, and expertise on how to bring our goals, dreams, and work to pass in this new era.

I am making it a priority to take extra time to pray and ask God for His specific strategies and solutions each day for me and my family. **Isaiah 2:3** says, **"He will teach us his ways, so that we may walk in his paths."** I believe He has a unique set of blueprints and a specific path marked out for each one of us. It may look impossible in the beginning, but He will show you how to overcome every obstacle and roadblock and face down every giant in your way. Pray that He makes His strategies clear to you and gives you courage and boldness to fulfill your assignment. I believe as you implement the right strategies, you will begin to see the way open up before you. I believe this will lead to success for not only you, but also for your family, your future work, business, and ministry, too.

As you take time to journal today, pray that God reveals His game plan to you. As you pray, write down whatever thoughts, ideas, or solutions that come to mind. Even write down what you have been thinking over recently and ask God to highlight which strategy you should implement next. Then pray for the courage to take the next right step and implement it in your life today.

Journal & Pray

God, I need a strategy and a blueprint to move forward in this area of my life . . .

____

____

____

As I pray, this solution and strategy come to mind . . .

____

____

____

God, please show me the next right step and how I can begin to implement this strategy in my life this week . . .

____

____

____

Day 37

Trust God's Perfect Provision

Breathing deeply, I exhaled a prayer and walked into the dance studio on Chicago's west side.

Weeks earlier, I had auditioned and been chosen for the Sally's Beauty Supply Dance Team. This may sound fabulous and easy to those professionally trained to dance. However, I was not. The reality of my inexperience sent fresh waves of anxiety over me as I walked through the door to rehearsal that first day.

Do you feel like you are stepping into something so much bigger than you right now? Do you feel like you are incapable of handling the challenge, the new job, the new path without God's help? If you do, you are in good company. I felt that same way as we started our week-long rehearsal for the dance tour. *God if you called me, make a way. Help me to learn these dances and give me your grace.* If you feel like you are in over your head, congratulations! God is stretching you and preparing you for your new season and the new level of your destiny. You may never feel quite ready, smart enough, strong enough, or completely capable on your own.

Thankfully, on that first day of practice, our choreographer pulled me and two other girls aside. He told us that due to the size of the team and the structure of our faces, we had been chosen to be "The Face of Sally's" that year. Our faces would be uniquely painted, and we would do theatrical runway while the rest of the dancers performed their routines. When I heard those words, I exhaled a sigh of relief. God made a way for me to be on the team and gave me a role I felt challenged in but still capable of handling.

During times like these, when I am being stretched and don't know how things can work out, I pray God will provide the ram in the thicket. Sometimes it is a physical provision or the finances we need, other times it is a way out or wisdom to handle the situation. In **Genesis 22:13–14 "Abraham looked up and there in a thicket he saw a ram caught by its horns. He went over and took the ram and sacrificed it as a burnt offering instead of his son. So Abraham called that place The Lord Will Provide. And to this day it is said, 'On the mountain of the Lord it will be provided.'"**

As you take time to journal today, pray about the fear

and insecurities that are holding you back from stepping out. Be honest as you confess your fears and ask Him to speak clearly to you. If you need wisdom, support, finances, or resources, ask for that too and believe He will provide *all* you need. Stand on the promises in His Word. No matter what you are facing, or how unprepared or under-resourced you currently are, rest assured The Lord Will Provide a way for you. Where God leads, He feeds. Where God guides, He provides. He will make a way where there seems to be no way.

Journal & Pray

God, I pray You would come alongside me as I take steps and move forward in what You have called me to do. Today, I need You to provide . . .

____

____

____

As I am praying and journaling today about these needs, I sense You are asking me to or leading me to . . .

____

____

____

Day 38

Partner with God

I lay there with an ice pack on the right side of my face. As if the infected root canal and the extracted tooth were not enough, now I was having extreme pain when I should have been healing. We were one month into the pandemic, and they had just opened my dentist's office for emergencies.

Suddenly, my phone rang. It was my childhood friend, Robyn, calling from Minnesota. She asked how I was feeling after she saw my Facebook post and I told her I was still in pain.

"Amy Esther, I think you have a dry socket. My sister Amy is a hygienist as you know, and she has seen a lot of these in patients at her dentist's office . . ."

Perhaps that explained why I still hadn't healed, even after two rounds of antibiotics. After I hung up the phone, I called the dentist right away with this new information and prepared for yet another visit. Just as Robyn predicted, I had a dry socket. It took several treatments to heal the tooth and soothe the nerve. A dry socket sends an excruciating, piercing pain from the source of your tooth up the side of your jaw to your ear. And in my case, it also went from the tooth to the front of my mouth and even under my tongue. I ended up going to the dentist eight times over two months for two separate tooth issues and I saw all five of the female dentists that worked in the practice. I also received a couple of nighttime calls from one of the dentists, as they checked in to make sure I was still functioning.

As crazy as those first couple of weeks were with constant throbbing, piercing pain, icing, and resting, I had a perfect opportunity to hear from God. He had a captive audience since I couldn't work much, exercise, or do my normal daily activities. It was during this time I discovered His heart and heard His direction for my life. Since my word for the year was "surrender" and my normal, steady, pay-the-bills job doing trade shows no longer existed due to COVID-19, I was all ears.

God impressed on my heart to partner with Him on the projects He was calling me to do. At the beginning of 2020, He gave me the idea to do video interviews, but I hesitated, feeling unprepared and ill-equipped. He reminded me that I already knew several directors for local charities, ministries, foundations, and non-profits. So, I started with those, and about six weeks after the initial tooth pain, my podcast *Support Someone Saturday* was birthed. God will often take your greatest pain and use it to birth your greatest purpose!

A second project God put on my heart to complete is the prayer journal you are reading right now. I have cried out to God in prayer through a lot of challenging seasons our family has gone through. God reminded me in **Psalm 81:7 (NKJV), "You called in trouble, and I delivered you; I answered you in the secret place. . ."** My prayer is that God ignites your faith and gives you fresh hope as you read how God answered prayers for my family. I know what He has done for us, He will do for you.

Today, as you pray and reflect on your own life and season, what do you hear Him speaking to you, and what do you sense the Holy Spirit is leading you to do? Perhaps you are one prayer, one step, or one challenge away from seeing your breakthrough. Don't give up! Keep trusting and partnering with Him, and He will see you through.

Journal & Pray

God, as I am reading and praying right now, I hear You speaking to me about . . .

____

____

____

The fears and the questions that are keeping me from stepping out are . . .

____

____

____

Here is how I plan to overcome these fears, so I can step out in faith into what You are calling me to . . .

____

____

____

Day 39

Find a Prayer Partner

As I transitioned from managing the teen center into a career in the modeling industry, I prayed God would strengthen me, equip me, and send people to pray me through. Support and community were essential as I launched out into the new!

Just a few years earlier, I graduated from Christian Life College with a degree in Pastoral Studies. My heart longed for others to come to know Jesus personally. I desired to bring His love into the modeling world. The new assignment I was walking into was so much bigger than me, but I also knew it was from Him.

"Amy, I believe God is going to bless you, grant you favor, open doors no man can shut, hide your weaknesses and imperfections, and make a way where there seems to be no way."

I nodded in agreement and listened intently as

Annabel, my newfound prayer partner spoke words of faith and blessing over my life. Not only had God brought me a woman who had great faith, but she also had experience in the fashion industry. She had worked as a designer in England. She knew the demands of the business and the expectations to be physically flawless as a model.

"And it doesn't matter how old you are; His gifts and His callings are irrevocable. He has called you into the modeling industry and He will make a way for you there. You are blessed and you are successful! Keep trusting Him," she admonished me.

Those life-giving words were salve to my weary soul as I launched into unfamiliar territory. I was almost thirty years old and just starting a full-time modeling career. Annabel had been an answer to my prayers and, in turn, I prayed for her as she worked to complete her Pastoral Studies degree. My prayers may not have had the same depth and breadth, but God sees our hearts, knows our thoughts, and listens to our prayers whether they are spoken with boldness or brokenness. **Matthew 18:19 (NKJV)** says, **"Again I say to you that if two of you agree on earth concerning anything that they ask, it will be done for them by My Father in heaven."**

There is power in prayer and there is power in partnership. When we come into agreement, God hears and answers our prayers. Psalm 133 reminds us when we walk in unity as brothers and sisters, there He commands the blessing, even life forevermore. He desires for all of us to be in community and to have people with whom we can share our hearts, find accountability, and grow in our faith walk with the Lord. God continues to answer my prayers and has blessed me with many different women I have prayed with in person, over the phone, through text messages, and over Zoom during different seasons of my life. There are amazing benefits of going to others during times of need and also being there for those who need a partner to agree with over a situation they are facing. It is exciting to see prayers answered all around, and it is faith-building to come into agreement and see God answer prayer in ways you never expected.

If you don't already have a prayer partner in your life, I encourage you to pray for the right one. Pray and ask God to show you a potential person to invite into your prayer life. Maybe that person has been praying for someone to come alongside them, too.

As you journal, I encourage you to write a prayer for your prayer partner, if you already have one. If you don't have a partner yet, write a prayer to God and ask Him to reveal to you the right person or people. I believe some of my greatest accomplishments have happened in life due to the power of praying with others and seeing God answer our prayers. I believe prayer moves mountains!

Journal & Pray

My prayer for my prayer partner today is...

____

____

____

God, I ask that You would bless . . .

____

____

____

God, please reveal to me a potential prayer partner, and show me who I can pray for in return today . . .

____

____

____

Day 40

It Is Finished

You? Write a book? Do you think anyone will read it? There are so many successful authors out there. What makes you think you can do this too?

Negative thoughts and insecurity bombarded my mind as I stepped out in faith to write my memoir. I didn't have experience or go to school for writing. I beat myself up for foolish mistakes I made when I was younger, along with the bad decisions and resulting consequences. Shame and lies clouded my mind as I endeavored to write . . . *If only I had a more stable upbringing and lived a more solid life, I would be a lot further along and more qualified to write my story.* Yet, this was not the way God saw me. The truth is, He completely redeemed my past. He called me into the modeling industry. He called me to write my book. He called me to model His behavior in the industry and now He was calling me to model my faith in Christ. He wanted me to share my story and let everyone know my secret weapon to success is really Him. My identity in Christ qualified me to do what He was asking, not my perfection—or lack of, for that matter. To move forward, I had to let go of doubt and shame and step out in faith and in His power.

Maybe you feel like you deserve to suffer or be in the doghouse, even though God has forgiven you. The problem is, when you punish yourself for your mistakes and sins, you are taking away the work of the Cross. Jesus died on the cross for you and me. He took our sin upon Himself. He took the punishment upon Himself so that you and I are completely forgiven and set free. If you continue to beat yourself up with shame and regret, you are negating what Jesus did for you on the cross. You are saying what Jesus did was not enough and that you still need to punish yourself. If you believe those lies, you will miss out on the call of God in your life. You will miss out on the freedom He has to offer you and the destiny He has for you. You need to ask God to forgive you, then forgive yourself and get back on the path He has for you. He wants us all to receive salvation, forgiveness, and the gift of Jesus Christ freely by faith. In **John 19:30**, right before Jesus died on the cross, He said, **"It is finished."**

As God continues to bring healing and restoration in my life over the years, I continue to work hard to retrain my thinking and my thought processes. It is like reprogramming a computer and it takes time. Maybe you have been told a lie or felt like, "I will never amount to anything—I am so stupid," or "I have screwed up so bad that I can never make this right," or "It's too late. I can't make this happen in my life now," or "I am not ______ enough to pull this off in life. . . ." If so, I would encourage you to say out loud, "Stop!" as I learned from Norman Vincent Peale years ago through *The Power of Positive Thinking*.

After recognizing the lie or the negative thought and saying, "Stop!" I then speak the truth or opposite out loud[6] and add, in Jesus' name. So instead of thinking, "I am not smart enough to pull this off—I can never write and publish a book," I say out loud, "Stop! I am smart enough and I have what it takes to write and publish a book. It WILL be done in Jesus' name." As you start to speak the truth out loud and agree with God's will to be done in your life, your faith and confidence grows, and you will start moving forward in the promises He has for you.

Take His promises with you today. Your sin, shame, and guilt over past mistakes are finished. Your self-doubt, insecurity, and inferiority based on your past are finished. Trust in His finished work on the cross for you. As you journal, work on creating new thought processes to reprogram your mind to think based on who you are in Christ and not who you were in the past. Come back to this daily, and follow up by reading and declaring who you are in Christ as listed in the appendix of this book. Remember, the moment you confess your sins, they are forgiven and covered in the blood of Jesus. See yourself clothed in His righteousness and purity and step into the new season He has for you in faith, freedom, and forgiveness.

Journal & Pray

God, take all the lies, negative thoughts, and wrong thinking I have believed over the years and set me free from them in Jesus' name. I ask that you help me replace these thoughts with the truth found in Your Word. Please help me to reprogram my thinking from this day forward, in Jesus' name.

When I think I am __________________________, then I will remember You said I am ______________________________.

When I am bombarded with this thought or lie:

____

I will stand on this verse (s):

____

____

As I pray about reprogramming my thinking, I want to make a list of who I am from your perspective. In Jesus Christ, I am:

____

____

____

CONCLUSION

You did it! Congratulations on praying through 40 days. My prayer is that you are unstuck, off the sidelines, and no longer circling the same mountain. I hope that you are on a new path moving toward the destiny that God has for you. My prayer is that God continues to strengthen you daily and that you stand firm in your identity in Christ and the authority and promises He has given you in His Word. I pray that God strengthens you to courageously take the next right step into your Promised Land. Don't stop and don't quit. I look forward to seeing you there.

Father God, touch everyone who is reading this right now. Lord, please strengthen us all as we have been weary. Give us a second wind, a fresh touch from You, and fill us with Your power and Your Spirit. Grant each one of us divine wisdom, strategies, and solutions to overcome obstacles and to move successfully forward in the plans that

You have for our lives. Make each one of our paths clear, and give us renewed motivation and stamina to implement the strategies You have given us.

Lord, thank You for bringing key people into each one of our lives who will help us move forward into the destiny You have for us. And while we are taking the next right step, let us look around and see who could use our helping hand. May we all continue to grow, go in the direction you are leading and give generously along the way. Let us all be like Joshua and Caleb—give us a clear vision of the Promised Land. Let us not dwell on the giants but rather look at the plush land, flowing with milk and honey. May we courageously and boldly go after all You have for us. I pray we all have wisdom, grace, and faith to take the land.

Let us all rest securely in our identity and our authority in Jesus Christ. Fill us all with bold faith to believe You for the impossible. Let us remain expectant and convinced You will help us to overcome every obstacle. I pray we choose to take the next right step every day until we enter our new season. We thank You in advance for Your strength and victory. Lord, use our story for Your glory. We love You Jesus, and we want to make Your name famous. Thank You for hearing and answering our prayers. In Jesus' name, we pray, Amen.

"Be strong and very courageous. Obey all the laws Moses gave you. Do not turn away from them, and you

will be successful in everything you do. Study this Book of the Law continually. Meditate on it day and night so you may be sure to obey all that is written in it. Only then will you succeed. I command you—be strong and courageous! Do not be afraid or discouraged. For the Lord your God is with you wherever you go." (Joshua 1:7-9 NLT/CE)

APPENDIX

Identity In Christ & His Promises
Daily Prayer & Declarations

Jesus, thank you that . . .

I am forgiven.
In him, we have redemption through his blood, the forgiveness of sins, in accordance with the riches of God's grace. (Ephesians 1:7, NIV)

I am a new creation.
Therefore, if anyone is in Christ, the new creation has come. The old has gone, the new is here! (2 Corinthians 5:17, NIV)

I am born again.
Jesus replied, "Very truly I tell you, no one can see

the kingdom of God unless they are born again. (John 3:3, NIV)

I am loved.

This is how God showed his love among us; He sent his one and only Son into the world that we might live through him. (1 John 4:9, NIV)

I am protected under your wings.

Whoever dwells in the shelter of the Most High will rest in the shadow of the Almighty. (Psalm 91:1, NIV)

I am safe in your care.

Even though I walk through the darkest valley, I will fear no evil, for you are with me; your rod and your staff, they comfort me. (Psalm 23:4, NIV)

I am an overcomer.

For everyone born of God overcomes the world. This is the victory that has overcome the world, even our faith. (I John 5:4, NIV)

I am fearfully and wonderfully made.

I praise you because I am fearfully and wonderfully made; your works are wonderful, I know that full well. (Psalm 139:14, NIV)

I am accepted in the beloved. (Beloved = Friends loved by God)

Having predestined us to adoption as sons by Jesus Christ to Himself, according to the good pleasure of His will, to the praise of the glory of His grace, by which He made us accepted in the Beloved. (Ephesians 1:5-6, NKJV)

I am written on the palm of your hands.

See, I have inscribed you on the palms of My hands; Your walls are continually before Me. (Isaiah 49:16, NKJV)

I am more than a conqueror.

No, in all these things we are more than conquerors through him who loved us. (Romans 8:37, NIV)

I am victorious over my enemies.

The Lord will extend your mighty scepter from Zion, saying, "Rule in the midst of your enemies!" (Psalm 110:2, NIV)

I am healed.

But He was wounded for our transgressions, He was bruised for our iniquities; The chastisement for our peace was upon Him, and by His stripes, we are healed. (Isaiah 53:5, NKJV)

I am restored.

So I will restore to you the years that the swarming locust has eaten, the crawling locust, the consuming locust, and the chewing locust, My great army which I sent among you. You shall eat in plenty and be satisfied, and praise the name of the Lord your God, who has dealt wondrously with you; and My people shall never be put to shame. (Joel 2:25-26, NKJV)

I am blessed with every spiritual blessing.

Praise be to the God and Father of our Lord Jesus Christ, who has blessed us in the heavenly realms with every spiritual blessing in Christ. (Ephesians 1:3, NIV)

I am always with You.

Keep your lives free from the love of money and be content with what you have, because God has said, 'Never will I leave you; never will I forsake you." (Hebrews 13:5, NIV)

I am no longer under condemnation; I am set free.

Therefore, there is now no condemnation for those

who are in Christ Jesus, because through Christ Jesus the law of the Spirit who gives life has set you free from the law of sin and death. (Romans 8:1, NIV)

I am close to You and secure in Your love.
For I am convinced that neither death nor life, neither angels nor demons, neither the present nor the future, nor any powers, neither height nor depth, nor anything else in all creation, will be able to separate us from the love of God that is in Christ Jesus our Lord. (Romans 8:38-39, NIV)

I am filled with Your peace.
Peace I leave with you; my peace I give you. I do not give to you as the world gives. Do not let your hearts be troubled and do not be afraid. (John 14:27, NIV)

I am filled with Your joy.
Nehemiah said, “Go and enjoy choice food and sweet drinks, and send some to those who have nothing prepared. This day is holy to our Lord. Do not grieve, for the joy of the Lord is your strength.” (Nehemiah 8:10, NIV)

I am able to overcome every temptation.
No temptation has overtaken you except what is

common to mankind. And God is faithful, he will not let you be tempted beyond what you can bear. But when you are tempted, he will also provide a way out so that you can endure it. (I Corinthians 10:13, NIV)

I am clothed with strength and dignity.
She is clothed with strength and dignity, and she laughs without fear of the future. (Proverbs 31:25, NLT)

I have hope and a future.
"For I know the plans I have for you," declares the Lord, "plans to prosper you and not to harm you, plans to give you hope and a future." (Jeremiah 29:11, NIV)

I have a vision from You, and it will come to pass in Your perfect time.
For the vision is yet for an appointed time; But at the end, it will speak, and it will not lie. Though it tarries, wait for it; Because it will surely come, it will not tarry. (Habakkuk 2:3, NKJV)

I have a faith that moves mountains.
"Truly, I tell you, if anyone says to this mountain, 'Go, throw yourself into the sea', and does not doubt

in their heart, but believes that what they say will happen, it will be done for them." (Mark 11:23, NIV)

I have forgiven all those who have wronged me.
And when you stand praying, if you hold anything against anyone, forgive them, so that your Father in heaven may forgive you your sins. (Mark 11:25, NIV)

I have faith that I will receive what I ask for in prayer.
Therefore I tell you, whatever you ask for in prayer, believe that you have received it, and it will be yours. (Mark 11:24, NIV)

I have the strength to do all things.
I can do all things through Christ who strengthens me. (Philippians 4:13, NKJV)

I have wisdom from above.
But the wisdom that is from above is first pure, then peaceable, gentle, willing to yield, full of mercy and good fruits, without partiality and without hypocrisy. (James 3:17, NKJV)

I have abundant provision.
Bring the whole tithe into the storehouse, that there

may be food in my house. "Test me in this," says the Lord Almighty, "and see if I will not throw open the floodgates of heaven and pour out so much blessing that there will not be room enough to store it." (Malachi 3:10, NIV)

I have power through Your Holy Spirit.

But you will receive power when the Holy Spirit comes on you; and you will be my witnesses in Jerusalem, and in all Judea and Samaria, and to the ends of the earth. (Acts 1:8, NIV)

I have a sound mind.

For God has not given us a spirit of fear, but of power and of love and of a sound mind. (2 Timothy 1:7, NKJV)

I have hope in You.

Now may the God of hope fill you with all joy and peace in believing, that you may abound in hope by the power of the Holy Spirit. (Romans 15:13, NKJV)

I have assurance you are working all things together for my good.

And we know that all things work together for good

to those who love God, to those who are the called according to His purpose. (Romans 8:28, NKJV)

I have love in my heart for others.
And hope does not put us to shame because God's love has been poured out into our hearts through the Holy Spirit, who has been given to us. (Romans 5:5, NIV)

I have kind words on my tongue.
She opens her mouth with wisdom, and on her tongue is the law of kindness. (Proverbs 31:26, NKJV)

I have the keys to guide my time in prayer.
I will give you the keys of the kingdom of heaven; whatever you bind on earth will be bound in heaven, and whatever you loose on earth will be loosed in heaven. (Matthew 16:19, NIV)

I have an open door before me.
I know your deeds. See, I have placed before you an open door that no one can shut. I know that you have little strength, yet you have kept my word and have not denied my name. (Revelation 3:8, NIV)

Final Homework

Now that you have finished working through this journal, I have one more assignment. Yes, you get extra credit. Take some time to look over your journal entries. What are 5 KEY MESSAGES God spoke to you? Write them here:

1. ______________________________

____

2. ______________________________

____

3. ______________________________

____

4. ______________________________

____

5. ______________________________

____

What are the 5 KEY STRATEGIES God gave to help you Step Into the New?

1. ______________________________

____

2. ______________________________

____

3. ______________________________

____

4. ______________________________

____

5. ______________________________

____

What 5 VERSES spoke the most to you? List them here and refer back to them, pray them out loud and stand on these promises as you enter your new season!

1. ______________________________

____

2. ______________________________

____

3. ______________________________

____

4. ______________________________

____

5. ______________________________

____

Use this extra space for journaling, writing prayers, and recording strategies. . .

ACKNOWLEDGMENTS

First of all, I want to thank you, Jesus, for rescuing me from a pit of destruction and despair when I was 21 and giving me a second chance at life. A special thank you to my husband Eric for your love, tireless support, weekly date nights, and loaning me the lobby at the AV3 Productions warehouse, so I could have space and solace to write this book! Thank you to Arianna and Ashton for your love, inspiration, motivation, and hard work at Zoom school, which in turn motivated me to work hard on this book.

Second, I want to give a special thanks to those who prayed for and encouraged me during the process of writing and publishing this book . . . Clara Barnes, Ella Louis, Lee Fisher, Kelly Tsoukalas, Farrah Hart Soppe, Sharon and Larry Martin, Dianne Matter, Donna Mall, Eleni Hanaris, Danielle Patelis, Janet Reich, Laura Zickert, Paige Adams, Mom and Dad Robnik, Mom and

Dad Joob, our Willow Family Small Group and so many more! I am sorry if I missed your name, please write it in here ________________________________.

I so appreciate all your prayers, encouragement, and support on this journey!

Third, thank you to those who helped with editing, proofreading, endorsing, and bringing this whole book to life. Thank you to my editor Becky Skillin, I could not have done this without you! Thank you, Becky Baudouin and Liz Lassa, for your endorsements, guidance, and direction with my manuscript and self-publishing. Thank you, Mindy Comincioli, for your fabulous cover design and David Edelstein for the formatting and wonderful book design. Thank you, Dad (Fred) Joob, Jean Johnson, Stacey Walgreen-Magnusson, Patti Petty, and Becky Baudouin for proofreading! Thank you for your words of affirmation and endorsement, Elissa Polley, Doc John Fuder, Marnie Swedberg, Rhonda Stoppe, Eldon Tracy, Carolyn Litton, and Larry and Jean Johnson. Thanks to Dr. Saundra Dalton Smith and Susan Neal for coaching me through this season of life and for loaning me your advice and expertise in so many areas!

Finally, I am so blessed by the wonderful community of folks at Willow Creek in Huntley and Chicagoland United in Prayer. A special thanks to our neighbors on

Ashley Street, including Kathy Heitkemper and Taryn Sarna as well as the Brown Family for carpooling and caring for our kiddos during this season as well. And last, but not least, a big shout out to our dog Blazer . . . thank you for your constant companionship and cuddling at my feet during the many hours I wrote, edited, and finalized this book.

THANK YOU, readers, the book launch team, and all those who picked up this book. I am so blessed and honored you chose to take the time to read and work through this prayer journal. I hope and pray it will truly transform your life, bless you and bring you to the next level of your destiny. Let's get UNSTUCK and step into the NEW together!

NOTES

1. Charles Bugg, "Stewardship" in Holman Bible Dictionary (Tennessee: Holman, 1991), 1303-1304.

2. Mark Batterson, All In: You Are One Decision Away from a Totally Different Life. (Zondervan, 2013), Kindle location 436.

3. Michael Chitwood, The Ability to Endure. Fayetteville, TX: The Runmotional Project, 2015.

4. Eugene H. Peterson, The Message: The Bible in Contemporary Language. (NavPress Publishing Group, 2002).

5. Merriam-Webster's Dictionary, Merriam-Webster.com, 2021.

6. Norman Vincent Peale, The Power of Positive Thinking (Simon & Schuster, 1980).

LET'S STAY IN TOUCH!

I'd love to hear from you about how this prayer journal has impacted your life. How have you gotten unstuck, what new steps are you taking, and how is God leading you? Feel free to reach out to me online and let me know!

If you'd like, you can check out my website, find a free minicourse on prayer and subscribe to receive my monthly newsletter. If you are looking for a speaker for your next event, either online or in person, you can contact me through my website. I look forward to connecting with you!

Website: www.amyjoob.com

facebook.com/AmyJoobAuthor

instagram.com/amyjoob1

YouTube: Amy Joob

linkedin.com/in/amy-joob-4466b226

May God bless you as you prayerfully take steps into the new!

Amy Robnik Joob

ALSO AVAILABLE FROM AMY ROBNIK JOOB

Available at Redemption-Press.Com and wherever books are sold.

Is God calling you to use the gifts He's given you to do something unique for Him? If God is calling you to an unconventional career, trust Him to lead you through every challenge, every difficulty, and every triumph. As Amy likes to say, "Bring it on, God! Let the adventure begin."

"In our contemporary world, with a shortage of positive role models, Amy Joob's voice rings true and needs to be heard. Young women searching for wisdom in finding their own unique career paths will find direction and encouragement in *Model Behavior.*"

—Becky Melby, co-author of *Spouse in the House*, Kregel Publishing

Made in the USA
Las Vegas, NV
06 January 2022

40384257R00125